Out of Zion

Lisa Brockman

HARVEST HOUSE PUBLISHERS
EUGENE, OREGON

Published in association with the literary agency of Wolgemuth & Associates, Inc.

Cover by Kara Klontz Design

Cover Images © Elena Pal , kilic inan, Boykov, Action Sports Photography, Boykov, Evelyn Chavez / shutterstock

Interior Salt Lake Temple Images © Pixabay

This book contains stories in which the author has changed people's names and some details of their situations in order to protect their privacy.

Out of Zion

Copyright © 2019 by Lisa Brockman
Published by Harvest House Publishers
Eugene, Oregon 97408
www.harvesthousepublishers.com

ISBN 978-0-7369-7645-9 (pbk.)
ISBN 978-0-7369-7646-6 (eBook)

Library of Congress Cataloging-in-Publication Data

Names: Brockman, Lisa, author.
Title: Out of Zion / Lisa Brockman.
Description: Eugene : Harvest House Publishers, 2019.
Identifiers: LCCN 2019015142 (print) | LCCN 2019021334 (ebook) | ISBN 9780736976466 (ebook) | ISBN 9780736976459 (pbk.).
Subjects: LCSH: Brockman, Lisa, 1969- | Protestant converts—United States—Biography. | Missions to Mormons. | Christian life. | Church of Jesus Christ of Latter-day Saints—Doctrines. | Mormon Church—Doctrines.
Classification: LCC BV4935.B657 (ebook) | LCC BV4935.B657 A3 2019 (print) | DDC 248.2/41409332—dc23
LC record available at https://lccn.loc.gov/2019015142

Printed in the United States of America

19 20 21 22 23 24 25 26 27 / BP-CD / 10 9 8 7 6 5 4 3 2 1

To Mom and Dad

We have journeyed through deep waters together.
I wouldn't have wanted to grow, weep, laugh, thrash,
and play in the depths with anyone else.

I love you.

Contents

A Note on Names

In August 2018, President Nelson, the current Prophet of the Church of Jesus Christ of Latter-day Saints, released a statement that members of the Church are no longer to use nicknames to refer to themselves, like Mormon or LDS. In October 2018, during the Church's worldwide General Conference, he stated, "The name of the Church is not negotiable. When the Savior clearly states what the name of His Church should be, and even precedes His declaration with 'Thus shall my church be called,' He is serious. And if we allow nicknames to be used and adopt or even sponsor those nicknames ourselves, He is offended."[1]

As a child growing up in the Church of Jesus Christ of Latter-day Saints during the 1970s and 1980s, I was proud to be a member of the Mormon Church and to be called a Mormon. Back then, it did not offend the Lord to call ourselves Mormons. Because this is the term we commonly used during the years in which my story was set, I will use that term throughout my book. I don't wish to disrespect anyone in using this term, but to use any other term would not be authentic to my story or the culture in which I was raised.

When One Question Shakes the Whole Foundation

I noted that it is sometimes hard to tell whether you are being killed or saved by the hands that turn your life upside down.[1]

BARBARA BROWN TAYLOR

*S*now fell white around us, blanketing earth with winter. Gary and I sat in his red Nissan 380ZX in front of the communications building. It was the close of the first semester of my freshman year at the University of Utah. A mutual friend on my tennis team had set up Gary and me on a blind date one month earlier, convinced we would click. We didn't just click—we were drawn together like magnets. Our personalities seemed to come even more alive when we were together, and our infatuation was mutual. We were both athletes and both living a bit rebelliously. Though we shared many commonalities, there was one very important reality we did not share—our religious beliefs. This tension between us was an ever-present reality that we chose to ignore for the first month of our relationship.

Two months earlier, I had been filled with excitement about leaving behind East High and venturing into a broader sea of people at the university. Although I was eager for my college experience, insecurity lurked. My friend, Kate, was attending the university as well, which was a relief. Having someone I knew and loved walking beside me into college life helped me not feel alone. Together, we decided to participate in Greek rush week. I romanticized Greek life due to all of the movies I had watched throughout high school and knew I would like to join a sorority.

On that hot Labor Day weekend, as Kate and I visited each sorority house on the first day of rush, I felt as though I were an object in a lineup being evaluated by a sea of beautiful young women. There were hundreds of freshmen rushing, all of us hoping to appear more mature than we were. My mind swam. How would I know if I was performing to their standards? There were so many of them. How could I appeal to enough of them to be chosen? In my attempt to hide my insecurity, I sang the songs the seasoned sorority girls taught me that day a little louder than usual and echoed sorority chants with gusto. I wondered what their criteria was for selecting who they would like to become their sister as I sat on benches in the Pi Phi house and belted out songs the song leader taught me. I envisioned the conversation the sorority sisters might be having that night: "She's okay. Maybe. She's perfect—we'll take her. But that one? No way, send her on to the next house."

On the final day of rush week, I found my home in Kappa Kappa Gamma. My entire body exhaled with the news that I had survived rush week and matched with a seemingly wonderful house of sisters. I had found my community for the next four years, my place of belonging.

The fall of my eighteenth year was full of goodness. My dream of playing college tennis, in spite of serious back injuries, had come true. Between the other athletes and sorority girls, I was making new friends. And Gary, a baseball player who looked like a god, was pursuing me. In my naïve vision of how college should be, I was living my ideal reality.

As Gary and I were getting to know each other, we talked briefly about our religious backgrounds. Though our lifestyles were incongruent with the tenets of our faith systems, we both possessed a deep conviction in the truth of our beliefs. I was a fifth-generation Mormon who had grown up in Utah in a devout Mormon family. We were members of the Church of Jesus Christ of Latter-day Saints and our religion permeated our lives. As long as I could remember, I wore the Mormon name with pride. Even during my short rebellion, my belief in Mormonism was unwavering.

Gary professed to be a Christian, but he didn't stop there. He said he was "born again." I was completely bewildered by that phrase. In my eighteen years of life, I had never before heard of someone calling himself "born again." I believed I was a Christian as well, but I didn't have a clue what "born again" meant. Gary had grown up in Idaho and attended a nondenominational Bible church…another foreign concept to me. Nondenominational? I didn't have a category for understanding the meaning of such a term.

Growing up in Utah in the 1980s as a Mormon meant that I lived a religiously sheltered life. I did know that there were Protestant and Catholic churches. One of my best friends in grade school was Jewish. And one of my closest friends in high school was Baptist and had an Amy Grant poster on his bedroom wall. But that was the extent of my knowledge about other religions. If my friends were not Mormon, they usually didn't practice any religion. It seemed like the Salt Lake area fostered the extremes of the religious spectrum. It was all or nothing.

From the beginning of our relationship, something about Gary that struck me as unique was that he talked about God and Jesus rather than his church or religion. I had never met anyone who talked so much about Jesus. He talked about Him with a familiarity that I had never encountered. It was so different from what I had always known about religion that it caught my attention. Yet, all the Jesus-talk was also a little annoying to me. At times, I felt strange for being annoyed that he talked so much about Jesus. Why would that annoy me? Mormons believed in Jesus. His name was in my church's name, after all. We talked about the Lord's goodness and provision, about the Spirit's promptings. But this was different. It was closer and extremely personal. I couldn't figure it out; I just knew that Gary's Jesus-talk was different from my experience, and that it was annoying.

I knew it was against my church rules to be dating a non-Mormon, and Gary knew he wasn't supposed to be dating me due to our differing faiths. But the connection between us was stronger than those beliefs, and our convictions didn't have the power to keep us apart at the time. We both knew our rebellion would be seasonal. One day, I would "clean up my act" and marry a Mormon in the Mormon Temple and he would marry a born-again Christian. But until that day came, we were glad to be wrapped up in each other.

As winter fell softly on a December day at the close of my first quarter, Gary drove me around campus to retrieve my grades. As he rolled the car to a stop, I grabbed the door handle to make my quick exit toward the communications building to pick up my report card. As I gripped the handle, Gary asked me a question. His words seemed to float across the space between us.

"How do you know Mormonism is true?"

Huh? I had never been asked that question before. I was focused on picking up my grades and beginning our winter break. Feeling whiplash, I turned to face him. His question was completely unexpected; however, I was prepared by my Mormon upbringing with an answer.

"Because I've experienced a burning in my bosom to confirm it's true," I said.

As a Mormon, I believed that if I asked Heavenly Father whether or not my church was true, I would know it to be the only true church on the face of the earth through a physical burning in my bosom.[2] I had felt the burning in my bosom time and time again as I was at church or youth events. Each physical and emotional experience affirmed my belief in Mormonism's truthfulness.

Gary was not so easily swayed. In fact, over the next fifteen minutes, he challenged my logic with intentionality. He asked me to tell him how a feeling alone makes something true and pointed out that feelings ebb and flow and are strongly influenced by our circumstances.

He was surprised that I would entrust my eternal destiny to emotional experiences alone. I, on the other hand, knew of no other paradigm for assessing the truth. I was taught to study Scriptures and the writings of the prophets. But in the end, a burning in my bosom, a feeling, was my plumb line for truth, and it had never occurred to me that this may not be the most valid standard of measure.

It had never crossed my mind to believe in any other way of *knowing* when it came to faith. I was taught not to question and test my beliefs throughout my childhood, so I never did. Since I was a little girl, I had been told stories of members in the church who had questioned their beliefs and were excommunicated from the congregation as a result. Faithful Mormons did not question and test their doctrine in any way but to ask for a burning inside them to validate it. Honestly, it had never occurred to me to question whether or not Mormonism was true. As long as I could remember, I had known that it was. I knew it in my deepest parts.

> What had felt like a firm foundation turned to quicksand beneath me.

Gary's curiosity had not been satiated with my answer to his first question. With care, he asked me several more.

"Have you looked into the historicity of Mormonism?"

Historicity? What was that?

"How do you know that Joseph Smith is a true prophet of God?" Gary asked.

"Because that's what I've been told and I believe it. I've experienced a burning in my bosom to validate it," I repeated. I began to feel uneasy.

"How do you know the Book of Mormon is God's Word?"

As Gary asked me legitimate questions, ones that had never crossed my mind, I grew more and more uncomfortable. The walls of the little sports car were closing in on me like a vice grip. Every instinct within me was to flee this conversation. I had never had a conversation of this nature before. Amid my discomfort, I quickly realized that a burning in my bosom wasn't going to convince Gary of anything. And that was my only argument. Adrenaline rushed through my body as I realized that I could not defend my beliefs with adequate responses. Within minutes, discomfort turned into panic. Mormonism was the only true church on the earth. We possessed the fullness of the gospel. All others were wrong. I had always believed those things wholeheartedly. Yet, it only took a few questions for me to see my ready defense was weak, at best.

What had felt like a firm foundation turned to quicksand beneath me. A space of painful isolation, void of the comfort or security I had possessed for eighteen years, opened inside of me. Over the next month, Gary and I continued to hang out together, but I avoided spiritual conversations. Nothing in me wanted to face my own ignorance or the possible weaknesses in my faith system. Challenging my beliefs would be a betrayal of my parents, my church, my community, and my family stretching back five generations. Yet, since Gary introduced me to questions that I had never entertained, a desire grew in me to be able to defend my religious beliefs.

What I Thought I Knew

One thing that brought me comfort was that deep down, I knew Mormonism was true. I knew it with all my heart. There might have been a chink in my armor of belief, but researching these questions to provide answers would only strengthen my faith. Perhaps that is what gave me the courage to eventually engage the questions that haunted me.

A month after that snow-blanketed day, as we began winter quarter, Gary courageously broke the unspoken silence I had enacted regarding the topic of our belief systems. Our affection for each other was growing, and if we were going to spend time together, we decided the most important area of our lives (even if it wasn't governing our choices at the time) needed to be addressed. We both believed the Bible to be the Word of God, so we agreed to study it together.

Actually, Gary believed *all* of the Bible to be true. I believed it to be true "as far as it was translated correctly."[3]

Mormons possess thirteen Articles of Faith, statements that summarize their fundamental beliefs. Joseph Smith, the founding prophet of Mormonism, penned them two years before his death, and they were the first set of truths I had been taught and had memorized as a child. Over and over I repeated this mantra: "We believe the Bible to be the word of God as far as it is translated correctly; we also believe the Book of Mormon to be the word of God." The caveat in this article of faith is that Mormons believe only Joseph Smith was given the personal revelation, capacity, and authority to translate the Bible correctly. Because I was a Mormon, this worked in my favor. We would use Joseph Smith's translation of the Bible to help us understand its meaning.

Although I had been taught the Scriptures my entire life, I had never possessed a burning desire to study them. As a Mormon, we only read the King James Version of the Bible because we believed that it was the most correct of all the translations. But I struggled to interpret the meaning of the words veiled in the antiquated language of the early 17th century. And I didn't know other versions of the Bible existed, nor would I have had the courage to read them if I had known. It felt like a betrayal to do so. But now, because I had never really studied the Bible or read it with the intention of defending Mormon doctrine, I decided it would be good to learn this ancient book's contents in greater depth.

As Gary and I moved toward Bible study, he introduced me to a world of biblical translations that was both bewildering and appealing. He showed me a Bible that had four different translations side by side. I was skeptical because it wasn't the King James, but I was also intrigued because I could understand what it was saying. With the King James and numerous other versions of the Bible in hand, we entered into Bible study. I hoped Gary would convert to Mormonism. He hoped I would encounter a Jesus he believed I had never met.

2

The Great Plan of Happiness

God orchestrates all of the influences in our life to blend
a symphony of themes that reflects his purposes.[1]

DAN ALLENDER

I was eight years old when I pulled my white baptismal gown over my head, anxiously awaiting my short journey to the font, where my beloved father, Melchizidek, priest in the Mormon Church, would take me by the hand and usher me into the lukewarm water. With one hand over my nose and the other gripping his forearm, pride filled my heart as I looked out onto the faces of people I knew and loved so well. My mom, siblings, extended family, and other church family looked on as loved ones—mostly eight years old, like me—were immersed into the cleansing waters.

"Lisa Halversen: Having been commissioned of Jesus Christ, I baptize you in the name of the Father, and of the Son, and of the Holy Ghost. Amen." As I squeezed my eyes shut, Dad plunged me into the water. I sank deep, making sure every part of me went beneath the surface. I wanted my baptism to be done right and every inch of me washed clean. When Dad pulled me up, my face gleamed, smiling ear to ear. I rubbed the water off my eyes and beamed with pride. I had dreamed of this day for years—the day when my name would be written on the rolls of the Church of Jesus Christ of Latter-day Saints. I was now a member of the Mormon Church.

My baptism was the first stone I laid in the foundation of my eternal destiny. It was up to me to make myself worthy of eternal life with Heavenly Father and Jesus Christ. I believed with all of my little heart in my own divine nature and my ability to earn that eternal life. What my eight-year-old imagination could never envision was how heavy this burden would become. But, on that day, I was center stage in a drama I had awaited ever since I could remember. I was covenanting with Heavenly Father to take upon myself the name of Jesus Christ, keep His commandments, and serve Him the rest of my life.[2] All of my sins were washed away, and I was now spiritually alive.

> From this day forward, I would be held accountable for my sins.

At church the following day, my dad took me by the hand and walked me to the front of the chapel. I sat down on a folding chair in front of the congregation while my dad, my grandpa, my uncle, my bishop, and his counselors placed one hand on each other's shoulders and the other on my head. I was privileged to sit in a chair in the circle of priesthood holders. I wore a pretty floral dress with lace trim all aglow, while my dad placed both of his hands lightly on top of my permed head. He prayed a priesthood blessing over me, confirming me as a member of the Mormon Church. He blessed me to receive the gift of the Holy Ghost, who would enable me to receive continual guidance and inspiration from Him if I was worthy. I would be worthy to receive His presence and gifts if I was earnestly seeking to obey Heavenly Father's commandments and keep my thoughts and actions pure. My sin slate had been washed clean of all the sins I had committed between the day I was born and my baptism. From this day forward, I would be held accountable for my sins.

Following my confirmation, I walked into Primary—church for children between three and eleven years old—holding my head a little higher than before. I sat down in a row with my cousin Heidi, and my other classmates, eager to tell everyone about my baptism while the teacher, Sister Kimball, worked to quiet the sea of children. Eventually, she got us all to assume our reverent prayer pose, crossing our arms in front of our bodies, bowing our heads, and closing our eyes. Sister Kimball opened us in prayer:

> Dear Heavenly Father, we thank Thee for this Sabbath day. We thank Thee that we can gather in church together to learn about Thee. We thank Thee for our families and friends. We ask that Thy Spirit will be with us so we can feel the Holy Ghost. We say these things in the name of Jesus Christ. Amen.

Then Sister Kimball led us in our opening hymn. We reverently sang "This Is My Father's World" and then recited the third Article of Faith: "We believe that through the Atonement of Christ, all mankind may be saved, by obedience to the laws and ordinances of the gospel."

After a lesson about our plan of salvation on the felt board, my favorite part arrived—twenty minutes of singing. We were like ticking time bombs aching to release the energy within us. We always had to be reverent in church, so we all loved when we could let our voices rip. With my left hand held out in front of me, palm up, I pounded down with my right fist as I belted out our first song:

> Book of Mormon stories that my teacher tells to me
> Are about the Lamanites in ancient history.
> Long ago their fathers came from far across the sea,
> Giv'n the land if they lived righteously.
>
> Lamanites met others who were seeking liberty,
> And the land soon welcomed all who wanted to be free.
> Book of Mormon stories say that we must brothers be,
> Giv'n the land if we live righteously.

We sang six more verses charting the big story of the Book of Mormon. Our songs were brilliantly crafted to plant the seeds of our doctrine deeply within our minds. Next we sang "Jesus Wants Me for a Sunbeam," popping up from our chairs each time we said "beam." Then, we sang "I'm a Mormon, Yes, I Am," "I Hope They Call Me on a Mission," and finished with "Families Can Be Together Forever." We covered all the important topics: Heavenly Father, Jesus Christ, Joseph Smith, our doctrines, and our church.

The Plan of Salvation

After sharing time, my class of eight-year-olds went into our own classroom for a lesson. A significant portion of my Primary lessons were about our plan of salvation, which we also called "The Great Plan of Happiness." My teachers diligently taught me that I was the offspring of Heavenly Father and Mother in a preexisting world, giving me a divine nature. While in that preexisting world, I chose Heavenly Father's plan, which meant I needed to come to this earth and gain a mortal body and then work out my eternal destiny by making myself worthy to be married in the Mormon Temple one day. It was a plan rooted in the value of people possessing free agency to choose whether or not we would follow Heavenly Father's plan for our lives. If I was faithful to keep the laws and ordinances of the Mormon gospel, I could make myself worthy to return to Heavenly Father and Jesus Christ in celestial glory after I passed from this life. I learned about my divine nature. I learned that God was once a man who, through His obedience, was able to work out His salvation and exalt into godhood. I was told that everybody who ever existed was given salvation, whether they accepted it or not. Jesus's death had wiped my soul clean of Adam's sin, so I entered this earth with an untarnished, sinless soul. I learned that Jesus's death and resurrection had saved me, that is, given me the ability to resurrect from the grave, and given me the option of eternal life depending on how I lived my life. I learned that at the center of the plan of salvation was family.

Our church was all about family. And I couldn't wait to be called "Mommy." Family was so central to our lives and religion because it was the vehicle through which our plan of salvation would be executed. We talked about family, family, and more family. As far back as my memory reaches, I dreamed of being married in the Mormon Temple to a fellow Mormon for time and eternity. I fantasized about it, hardly able to wait for that day. I determined to live as righteously as I possibly could so that one day, I would walk through the Temple doors alongside my husband-to-be, vowing to marry each other for time and eternity. There, I would exalt into a "goddess"[3] and my husband a "god," and I would birth spirit children throughout eternity.

> Family was the vehicle through which our plan of salvation could be executed.

This vision had been instilled in me from birth. My parents have always been devout, faithful Mormons. I come from a lineage of five generations of Mormons who have persevered in their faith for about 150 years. I was raised on stories of my ancestors who made their way to Utah and Idaho, some of whom lost children along the way due to the extreme conditions.

On Saturday nights, either my mom or dad would roll my hair around pink, spongy curlers, intent on infusing my toothpick-straight hair with curls for Sunday church services. We rarely missed church, whether we were in town or traveling. Our family was dedicated to keeping the Sabbath day holy, which meant we spent three hours of our Sundays in church services and refrained from playing with friends or doing much activity throughout the rest of the day. I always had to wear a dress or skirt and blouse alongside all of the women and girls in our ward, or local congregation. This felt like the worst kind of torture, given my tomboy personality and love for Levi Strauss 501 jeans and IZOD polos. The men sported suits and ties, white shirts (usually), and dress shoes. We believed modesty and dressing nicely showed respect for God in His home.

Sacrament Meeting

After two hours of Primary, I hurried to the chapel to look for my family. During the final hour of church, the entire congregation, including all of the children, worshiped together in the chapel in a service called Sacrament Meeting. Though it was meant to be a solemn time of worship, parents spent a good part of their energy keeping their kids entertained throughout the seventy-minute meeting. I now know Sacrament Meeting is an endurance test for parents with small children, who needed to keep them as quiet as possible and contained in their pew throughout a very non-child-friendly service. It would always bring uncontrollable giggles when one of the toddlers escaped the pew and ran down the aisle toward the stand where the bishopric sat. The bishopric consisted of three men who were lay leaders called to shepherd the congregation. The bishop was the leader and the other two men were his first and second counselors. I always thought the bishop and his counselors were especially righteous men, since they had been worthy to be called to lead our congregation.

During Sacrament Meeting, we sang hymns, partook of the sacrament, and usually listened to members of the congregation give talks. The partaking of the sacrament was led by the Aaronic priests in the ward—boys between twelve and eighteen years old who had been baptized and were living an upright life, making them worthy of holding the priesthood. During this part of the service, young men over sixteen years old would tear the white Wonder Bread while kneeling at the front of the chapel. The congregation would sing a song about our Savior while the bread was being prepared. By the close of the song, the young priests would retrieve the bread trays and pass them down each pew until everyone had been served. They would then follow with small cups of water, representing Christ's blood. The purpose of the sacrament was to cleanse us of the sins we had committed since we last partook of the sacrament. Each time we partook of the sacrament, we were renewing the covenants we made with Heavenly Father at our baptism.

The water we drank in the mini paper cups was a reminder that the Savior suffered in the garden of Gethsemane as He sweat blood in intense spiritual suffering and anguish for our sins. In the garden He said, "My soul is exceeding sorrowful, even unto death" (Matthew 26:38 KJV). Submitting to the will of the Father, He suffered more than we can comprehend: "Blood [came] from every pore, so great [was] his anguish for the wickedness and the abominations of his people" (Mosiah 3:7). "He suffered for the sins, sorrows, and pains of all people, providing remission of sins for those who repent and live the gospel. Through the shedding of his blood, Jesus Christ saved all people from what the scriptures call the 'original guilt' of Adam's transgression."[4] Remembering Christ's anguish in the garden of Gethsemane and His suffering on our behalf was central to Sacrament Meeting

Our church services were solemn affairs. We believed that only particular instruments were conducive to reverent worship, and Heavenly Father preferred reverent worship. The organ and piano were our staple instruments. Our hymns were all sung to the organ. The Church teaches that "music should be worshipful and fit the spirit of the meeting.... Music and musical texts are to be sacred, dignified, and otherwise suitable for sacrament meeting."[5] Classical instruments were acceptable in our services, but never would there be a drum set, electric guitar, or loud sounds. They would break the worshipful climate and were not pleasing to our God, at least when it came to worship. Basically, worship needed to be solemn enough that grandpas and teenage priests could sleep through parts of it, because this was a common occurrence.

All About Family

Family was central in our lives and religion. Former Brigham Young University professor Grant Von Harrison describes the weightiness of parenthood in the Mormon Church:

> Married couples are the authorized agents of God to create physical bodies for his spirit children. Bringing children

into mortality is a very sacred responsibility. In fact, there is nothing that is more sacred than the process of reproduction by which premortal spirits receive mortal bodies. When couples assume the role of creators they are just as responsible as God is for his creations....When we enter the marriage covenant, we should be willing to assume the responsibility of parenthood. If we are not willing to assume this responsibility, we should not get married. It is wrong to enter into marriage with the intent of postponing a family.[6]

Family is the context through which Heavenly Father's plan of salvation (the journey from being spirit children in the preexisting world to exalting into gods and goddesses in the Celestial Kingdom) would be executed. There is no greater fulfillment to faithful Mormons than successfully parenting their children.

My mom and dad were sealed for time and all eternity when they married in the Salt Lake Temple. Their marriage would last throughout eternity if they remained faithful to each other and the Temple laws and ordinances. Harrison captures the importance of a Temple marriage: "Of all the gospel ordinances, eternal marriage is the most important. We cannot be exalted if we are not sealed to our spouse in the next world. We must have a companion to share the honors and blessings of exaltation."[7] I learned at a very young age that eternal life was dependent on my marrying a Mormon man in the Temple one day. This was the central prerequisite in order to enjoy our Great Plan of Happiness. Because my parents married in the Temple, my siblings and I were *sealed* to them throughout eternity. During these formative years of my life, it was imprinted on my soul that Mormon parents' greatest hope was that all of their children would obtain Temple marriages and be eternally sealed to their spouses in the Temple. Families could be together forever if we followed Heavenly Father's plan.

One of the activities prescribed by the Church to strengthen families is called "family home evening." All around the world, Mormon families worked to be faithful to family home evening. On Monday nights, my dad would teach a short lesson, we would sing, play a game, and be together. As a small child, I loved family home evening. I had an older brother and a younger sister, and when I was twelve and fourteen, my parents added two more siblings to our family. It was a fun way to have our beliefs reinforced without having to dress up for it. And it was one night a week that we all played together. We believed Heavenly Father would bless us if we faithfully gathered for family home evening.

My dad took the centrality of family seriously when he was able to be home. His job as a physician was demanding, and as I entered my preteen years, he was mostly at work during my waking hours. However, when dad was home, he was all in. He would help with the bedtime routine, even rolling my long hair into the spongy rollers if needed. (Apparently, in the '70s this was a mandatory beauty regimen.) He loved reading us bedtime stories and tucking us into bed. He was my math tutor, he helped my mom with weekend meals, and he cultivated a beautiful garden. He even loved to mill the wheat and bake homemade bread.

My mom was committed to her calling as a wife and mother. Though she had earned a master's degree in business education, when her first baby entered this earth, she happily embraced her calling to motherhood. This is the ultimate call in a Mormon woman's life. She worked hard to keep our home a place welcoming to others, and she loved creating beauty. My mom sacrificed her life to provide opportunities for us to flourish in our God-given talents and abilities. She took great pride in our successes and felt our losses deeply.

Developing abilities is important to Mormons. I was taught that as a pre-mortal spirit, I was responsible to develop my gifts. I was offered unlimited opportunities to do so, and the degree to which I took initiative determined how much I would grow my abilities in the preexisting world. The innate abilities I possess at birth on this earth are determined by the investment I made to grow my abilities in the preexisting world. According to Brigham Young, "Human beings are expected by their Creator to be actively employed in doing good every day of their lives, either improving their own mental and physical condition or that of their neighbors."[8] Developing our abilities was central to our family culture.

I was almost constantly active in sports and music lessons. Mom drove me from lesson to lesson, committed to doing all she could to enable my talents to flourish. Thankfully, my dad was usually able to generate the resources needed to support her passion and mine. During a season of not-as-much-plenty, my mom taught piano lessons to generate income to pay for lessons. A few years ago, I laughed and told her, "I didn't even know you played the piano." Laughing in return, she replied, "Ya gotta do what ya gotta do." She was committed to her children having every opportunity to shine.

I've come to see how profoundly the objects of our worship rub off on us. With each day, we begin to resemble more and more whomever and whatever we worship. We take on our God's accent, likeness, gaze, and scent. During the formative years of my life as a Mormon girl, one of the ways my view of God shaped me was that I placed great value on family and the necessity of a Temple marriage. I also wanted to be a mother, to be called "Mommy" when I grew up—nothing else would do. I was inclined toward relationships with boys from a very early age, which I believe was influenced by the doctrine about marriage and family being the consummate good, the end toward which all should strive.

> We resemble whomever and whatever we worship. We take on our God's accent, likeness, gaze, and scent.

By the age of five, I began trying to find a sense of significance through relationships with boys. Another significant way my view of God formed me was a growing awareness that I needed to make myself worthy—for the presence of the Holy Ghost, for God's blessings, for a Temple marriage, and for eternal life. The weight of pursuing personal worthiness was stamped on my soul at a very early age.

When I was six years old, I was finally old enough to be given my "Choose the Right" ring. It was a ring that would fit my skinny little fingers and had a green shield with a CTR imprinted on it. It reminded me to choose the right each time my eyes swept past my ring. I wore it with pride. I loved having a special ring about which my friends and kids at school would ask whenever they noticed it. I liked being set apart as a Mormon. I liked that we were unique.

3

Worthy

Every human being is a mixture of light and
darkness, trust and fear, love and hate.[1]

JEAN VANIER

I took the microphone from the teenage priest who was transporting it between ward members who wanted to share their personal testimonies. Flanked by my mom, dad, older brother, and little sister, I stretched as tall as my eight-year-old frame could and bore my testimony in the sing-songy Mormon prayer voice to our church congregation: "I know the Church is true. I know Jesus Christ is the Son of God. I know Joseph Smith is a true prophet of God, I know the Book of Mormon is the Word of God. I say these things in the name of the Lord Jesus Christ. Amen."

I was an official member of the Church and was excited to proclaim my belief in these truths. It was the first Sunday of the month, which meant that all the members of our ward, or congregation, were to have fasted that morning in preparation for the fast and testimony meeting. As I entered the kitchen that morning, my stomach growled, expecting its usual "feast" of unsweetened Cheerios. Not this morning. I was a member of the Church and was now required to fast the first Sunday of each month. Three hours of church stood between me and my next meal. *How hard could this be?* I thought. Pride filled my little frame, my little floral dress with lace trim cloaked it, and my perfectly permed short hair topped it off. *This should be no big deal. It's just one meal,* I convinced myself.

Fasting would create the necessary sacrifice for an extra portion of the Holy Ghost to bring inspiration to my spirit. I felt pride that I was finally a member who was required to fast through church services that day, yet after I'd completed the first two hours of worship, struggling to focus on anything but my shrinking stomach, fasting didn't feel quite so novel. On fast Sunday, Sacrament Meeting was a kind of open-mic time with a very specific purpose: Members were to testify to what they *know* to be true about the Church. This was how we would encourage and build up one another's faith. During these meetings, we felt the Holy Ghost in many ways. Sometimes, He would cause a burning in our bosom or a warm sensation inside of us. Other times, He would stir deep feelings in our hearts. It was not uncommon to see grown men and women in tears during this meeting. All of these experiences worked to confirm our testimonies that Mormonism is the one and only true church of God on this earth.

As Mormons, personal testimony was the foundation upon which our faith was established. We were exhorted to build our testimonies through heartfelt prayer, Scripture study, and by living obediently the commands of our gospel. We were encouraged to "bear our testimonies" often, for this exercise helped strengthen our faith as well as that of others. Space was created in all our meetings and gatherings for the bearing of testimony, even in Primary. Dieter Uchtdorf, one of the current twelve apostles of the Mormon Church, describes testimony this way: "When we talk about testimony, we refer to feelings of our heart and mind rather than an accumulation of logical, sterile facts. It is a gift of the Spirit, a witness from the Holy Ghost that certain concepts are true."[2]

The pervasive sharing of testimony in the Church is based on two central beliefs. The first is that the primary responsibility of members is to "teach one another"[3] rather than to depend upon one formal teacher or minister only. The second is that the power that motivates individuals to live as Christ taught is the power of the Holy Ghost, rather than the power of logic or the eloquence of gospel teachers. My testimony was not based on rational thought or persuasive teaching, but rather was the fruit of the Holy Ghost revealing the truth of the tenets of our gospel to me through personal inspiration.

Brigham Young, the second prophet of the Mormon Church, described how he had been converted to Mormonism through witness, not facts:

> If all the talent, tact, wisdom, and refinement of the world had been sent to me with the Book of Mormon, and had declared, in the most exalted of earthly eloquence, the truth of it, undertaking to prove it by learning and worldly wisdom, they would have been to me like the smoke which arises only to vanish away. But when I saw a man without eloquence, or talents for public speaking, who could only say, "I know, by the power of the Holy Ghost, that the Book of Mormon is true, that Joseph Smith is a prophet of the Lord," the Holy Ghost proceeding from that individual illuminated my understanding, and light, glory, and immortality were before me. I was encircled by them, filled with them, and I knew for myself that the testimony of the man was true.[4]

Even as an eight-year-old girl, I believed that my testimony of the Mormon Church was known through personal inspiration via the Holy Ghost, often manifested in a burning in my bosom. I wanted to be worthy of the Spirit touching me as often as possible. For Mormons, no amount of learning, reasoning, or logic could outweigh the value of personal testimony as a source of knowing truth. I possessed a deep knowledge that personal testimony that was the result of inspiration from the Holy Ghost, and inspiration trumped all other ways of knowing whether or not my church was true. Though my testimony was young, it was precious to me and was something to share frequently with pride.

After I sat down, one by one members rose and testified to the truth of Mormonism. Usually, members shared a story of how the Spirit was strengthening their testimony, either through crisis or provision. I remember a woman who shared how a family member had been burned in a car accident and everywhere but where her garments covered her body was burned to a crisp. (Garments are underwear worn only by active Temple-attending members of the LDS Church.) Her garments had protected her from the flames.

If garments have that kind of power, I want to wear them, I thought as she cried through her story. *I'll have to wait a long time to get them…I hope I don't get in a fire before that. I won't have garments to protect me from the flames.*

From young to old, those present were welcomed to testify to others. We feasted on the Holy Ghost's presence and opened our hearts to the burning inside, which was confirmation that we were living in a manner worthy of visitation. I really liked fast Sunday because it was a change from the usual meeting of prepared talks and was filled with spontaneity. Fasting, on the other hand, wasn't as enjoyable as my eight-year-old mind had hoped. But I knew Heavenly Father would bless me if I remained obedient to His command to fast one day a month.

Now that I had been baptized and was a member of the Church, it was my responsibility to begin laying the foundation for my eternal destiny—the Celestial Kingdom. I was to prepare myself for a Temple marriage. My preparation included active church participation, paying a full tithe, staying morally pure, obeying the Word of Wisdom, serving others, and living a life of integrity. My obedience to the laws and ordinances of the gospel would open me to greater inspiration from the Spirit and strengthen my testimony.

I was diligently taught the law of tithing. Under this law, I was commanded to tithe ten percent of my income to the Church, which is called a "full tithe." Though my earning potential as a young girl wasn't great, I remember collecting the coins I occasionally earned and dropping them into my cardboard tithing bank, which had separate compartments for spending, saving, and tithing. By the time I was ten years old, I was able to mow our lawn, which earned me ten dollars per week. I faithfully deposited my tithing portion into my little bank. Once a month, I filled out a paper slip available in the foyer at church, filled in my name and amount of tithe enclosed, and placed it into the tithing box. Pride filled my little heart each time I gave my tithe to my bishop. I wanted to *choose the right*.

I was taught that if I faithfully tithed, I would be blessed. A former president of the Church said, "I appeal to the Latter-day Saints to be honest with the Lord and I promise them that peace, prosperity and financial success will attend those who are honest with our Heavenly Father."[5] I desired the blessings I would reap from my obedience. In addition, I was the kind of girl who really wanted to do the right thing.

In December, the time came for my first tithing settlement. I had not been required to tithe until I became a member of the Church. My entire family walked into our bishop's office, where the bishop had a printed report of the amount each of us had tithed on his desk. One by one, he addressed each of us as we sat across from him.

"Brother and Sister Halversen, you have tithed ____. Is this a full tithe?"

"Yes, it is," responded my mom and dad.

Next he addressed my older brother. "Is this a full tithe?"

"Yes, it is," said my brother,

It was my turn. I sat forward in my chair, eager to know how much I had given that year.

"Lisa, you have tithed ____. Is this a full tithe?"

"Yes! That is a full tithe."

My little sister wasn't required to tithe yet because she was only six. We had all obediently kept the law of tithing that year, and we left the bishop's office with humble hearts. At least, we were supposed to leave humbly. Inside I felt a burst of pride.

The tithing settlement helped keep us accountable to the Law of Tithing. In order to marry in the Temple, I needed to pay a full tithe. If I wasn't paying a full tithe, my sin would disqualify me from being Temple-worthy. So, though I was young, I was forging habits that would help create a solid foundation for my eternal destiny in the Celestial Kingdom. At nine years old, these commands didn't feel that strenuous. It was like I was picking up pebbles of faithfulness and placing them in my eternal foundation. I wanted to receive all the blessings possible. And I wanted to be worthy of Heavenly Father's acceptance, presence, and love.

Prophet Spencer W. Kimball, our prophet during my girlhood, spoke these words:

> If we…keep the commandments with all our heart as did Hezekiah, the Lord will guide us through troublous times, and we shall gratefully see his help in our behalf, and we will give deep love and appreciation to him for his many kindnesses and goodnesses. He is our Lord and our Great Strength. If we are *worthy*, he will be there in our time of need. Of that I have a sure understanding.[6]

I wanted to be worthy of Heavenly Father's presence in my times of need. Everything in me wanted to be worthy.

The Priesthood

One honor I knew I would never be worthy of was holding the priesthood. Only men could hold the priesthood, in which resides all authority in the Mormon Church. When I was nine years old, my older brother turned twelve, making him old enough to receive the Aaronic Priesthood. Like in the Old Testament of the Bible, we believed priests were Heavenly Father's agents on this earth and vehicles of His healing power and authority for His people. We believed that within four hundred years of the last of Jesus's apostles passing away, His Church passed away, a phenomenon we called the Great Apostasy. The Mormon Church explains it this way:

> With the death of the Apostles, priesthood keys, or the presiding priesthood authority, were taken from the earth.

> Without these watchmen—the Apostles who had kept the doctrines of the gospel pure and who maintained the order and standard of worthiness in the Church—the members faced serious challenges. Over time, doctrines were corrupted and unauthorized changes were made in Church organization and priesthood ordinances.[7]

According to Mormon teaching, Joseph Smith brought back the priesthood. I was taught that he had a visitation from John the Baptist who conferred the priesthood upon him and Oliver Cowdery, the co-translator of the Book of Mormon. The Mormon priesthood was superior to all other earthly priesthoods because it was not passed down generationally or acquired through education but came directly from John the Baptist. Smith restored the Aaronic and Melchizedek Priesthoods to the earth through Mormonism.

Priesthood holders embody authority in the Church—the authority of God delegated to men. My brother Lane was now of age and found worthy by our bishop to receive the Aaronic Priesthood. He would be qualified to participate in sacred priesthood ordinances. My dad and our bishop, as well as other men in the church, laid hands on Lane's head during the priesthood quorum meeting and conferred upon him the Aaronic Priesthood. I did not get to see it happen because only men and boys are allowed in the priesthood meeting. He was made a deacon, which enabled him to serve the sacrament each Sunday in Sacrament Meeting. This was a high honor for a teenage boy. If he lived worthily, he would gain greater priesthood authority, becoming what we called a teacher at the age of fourteen and a priest at the age of sixteen. Then, at the age of eighteen, if he was worthy, the Melchizidek priesthood would be conferred upon him, which is greater than the Aaronic priesthood. Each office of the priesthood offered greater levels of opportunity to perform priesthood ordinances. Priesthood ordinances include administering baby blessings, baptisms, ordinations, the sacrament, priesthood blessings, and blessings for healing.

The lowest office of the Melchizidek Priesthood is elder. Before my brother would leave on his two-year mission for the Church, he would be ordained an elder. Elders are ministers of Christ. The other four offices in the Melchizidek Priesthood are high priest, patriarch, seventy, and apostle, each one carrying greater authority and position in the Church. The Quorum of the Seventy and the Twelve Apostles work closely with the Prophet to carry out Heavenly Father's work around the world. When one of these seats becomes unpopulated through death or another reason, the Church fills that seat with another worthy man so that these positions of leadership are always occupied. One of the Twelve Apostles, David Bednar, states,

> As we do our best to fulfill our priesthood responsibilities, we can be blessed with priesthood power. The power of the priesthood is God's power operating through men and boys like us and requires personal righteousness, faithfulness, obedience, and diligence. A boy or a man may receive priesthood authority by the laying on of hands but will have no priesthood power if he is disobedient, unworthy, or unwilling to serve.[8]

For men and boys to remain worthy priesthood holders was critical to our faith.

The greatest blessings a Mormon man can receive in this life are associated with the priesthood. On the day my brother received the priesthood as a twelve-year-old boy, he possessed more authority than my mother or any of the women in the Church. For so long, I believed men were special because they were worthy to hold priesthood authority. Women were to humbly come under their leadership. Men held the keys to the Kingdom of God and women were dependent upon them to enjoy those blessings—even exaltation into godhood.

The Mark of Cain

A significant issue in the Mormon Church during my Primary years was that black people were not allowed to hold the priesthood

or participate in the Temple ceremonies, such as the endowment ceremony, marriage ceremony, and family sealings (for time and eternity).
This prevented them from possessing authority in the Church as well
as from participating in the Temple ordinances that were essential to
eternal life or exaltation into godhood. I was taught the biblical story
of Adam and Eve, who had two sons, Cain and Abel. Out of jeal-
ousy, Cain murdered Abel. God cursed Cain with a mark. Mormons
believed that this mark was black skin.[9] As a result, black people were
not allowed to access the blessings offered white people. I had also
been taught that black people had not been as valiant in the preexisting world and were cursed as a result. In addition to these beliefs
about black people, I learned about the Lamanites, a Latin American
people group in the Book Mormon who descended from an evil Isra-
elite and thus had darker skin.

But this teaching came to an end. June 9, 1978, was a monumental day for the Mormon Church. General Conference, our semi-
annual worldwide conference, was in session. It was three days filled
with talks, mostly from the prophet and apostles. My parents and
the adult members of the Church eagerly await hearing directly from
our prophet and apostles. For me, it meant church on Saturdays as
well as Sundays, which in my opinion was too much! Three hours on
Sunday felt like plenty to me. This General Conference marked the
end of an era. The prophet, Spencer W. Kimball, and his twelve apostles had received inspiration from Heavenly Father that black people
were now worthy to receive the priesthood and participate in all of
the Temple ceremonies. They would be given the privilege of holding
the priesthood and participating in the Church ordinances that only
white people had been blessed to enjoy for the previous 150-plus years
of the Church's existence. Apostle Bruce R. McConkie described the
process he and the other Church leaders went through when receiving the revelation:

> President Kimball knew, and each one of us knew, inde-
> pendent of any other person, by direct and personal

revelation to us, that the time had now come to extend the gospel and all its blessings…to those of every nation, culture, and race, including the black race…. It was a revelation of such tremendous significance and import; one which would reverse the whole direction of the Church…. The Lord could have sent messengers from the other side to deliver it, but he did not. He gave the revelation by the power of the Holy Ghost. Latter-day Saints have a complex: many of them desire to magnify and build upon what has occurred, and they delight to think of miraculous things. And maybe some of them would like to believe that the Lord himself was there, or that the Prophet Joseph Smith came to deliver the revelation, which was one of the possibilities. Well, these things did not happen. The stories that go around to the contrary are not factual or realistic or true…. I cannot describe in words what happened; I can only say that it happened and that it can be known and understood only by the feeling that can come into the heart of man. You cannot describe a testimony to someone.[10]

This was a radical shift in our religion. At the time, it did not affect me personally because we didn't have any black people in our neighborhood or in our ward (that I remember), and only a few attended my school. But I remember it being a huge day for our church, nevertheless. What I did not know was that at eight years old, already deeply rooted within me was our belief that black people were black because of the curse of Cain and were, therefore, not worthy of the same blessings white people enjoyed. It would take years—not until I moved out of Utah—before I became aware of the effects of racism in my heart and mind and the stereotypes ingrained in me, stereotypes that were diminishing to people of color. This root needed to be exposed and yanked out of my soul.

The Prophet and Modern-Day Revelation

I revered our prophet, Spencer W. Kimball. He was God's mouthpiece for us. He was a spiritual giant who was a mediator between

Heavenly Father and Church members, much like Moses. He was our seer, receiving new revelation from God and testifying about Jesus Christ and His gospel, making known His will and character. With boldness, our prophet denounced sin and warned us of its consequences. He would even prophesy of future events. I was warned that those who did not follow the prophet's teachings would fall and that if I obeyed him, I would be blessed.[11] It never occurred to me to ever question his revelations or any of his decisions. I admired and respected Spencer W. Kimball. If he had told me to jump, I would have asked, "How high?"

Modern-day revelation and inspiration were unique to our faith and was something that made us different from most religions. We were the only church on the earth since Christ who had prophets and apostles leading us as seers and revelators. I believed that Heavenly Father had the freedom and desire to actively evolve our doctrines and teachings, which is how the Book of Mormon came to be. As a result, we humbly claimed that our church alone possessed the "fullness of the gospel." I felt toward the prophet what I thought I would feel one day toward my husband in the Celestial Kingdom when he was a god and I his queen and high priestess—awe.

Love-Hungry at Eleven

Throughout the fifth and sixth grades, I was completely enamored with Finn Price. He was a blond-haired, blue-eyed preppy boy who dressed in Polo shirts, Levi's 501 jeans, and Sperry Top Siders sock-free. To my delight, this was not a one-sided crush—he also had a crush on me. I could not wait to see him at school in the mornings and sit with him through class all day long. Providence saw to it that we were in the same class throughout the fifth and sixth grades.

Finn was one of the sources of my identity. It was amazing to feel worthy of a boy's acceptance and affection just for being me. I fantasized about marrying him one day. Marriage was such a common topic of conversation in our Mormon lives that I could not help but long for it and idealize it. Finn was not a Mormon, and I was only supposed to reserve my affections for Mormon boys, but I was so young and so far away from marriage that I didn't care.

Valentine's Day

Saturday night had finally arrived. I had anxiously awaited this night for two weeks. I was hosting my first Valentine's Dance. Mom had prepared the refreshment table with a heart-covered paper tablecloth and a Raggedy Ann and Andy honeycomb paper centerpiece. She had at least one paper honeycomb centerpiece for every holiday including Presidents' Day. She loved celebrating holidays and events. I pulled on my Levi's 501 jeans, ruffled striped dress shirt, and Sperry Top-Siders, finishing off my stellar outfit with a white ribbon that I tied around my collar. I curled my hair to mimic Dorothy Hamill's, put the finishing touches on the decorations, and made sure my music playlist was ready to go with tapes of Kenny Rogers and Neil Diamond. What more could we need for a fifth-grade dance? My friends filtered in until there were about fifteen of us. And then there was Finn—my valentine decked out in khaki pants, a Polo sweater and of course, Sperry Top-Siders.

We turned our unfinished basement into a dance venue with a massive group of eleven-year-olds moving and grooving to our hearts' delight. And then my dream came true. As Neil Diamond belted out "Love on the Rocks," Finn wrapped his arms around my waist while I wrapped my arms around his neck. Our swaying back and forth to the rhythm of the music resembled a Frankensteinian stagger. Slowly, we danced toward a little private space between two doors leading out to my garage. Finn's soft lips pressed against mine and I would have been glad for the song to have lasted for the rest of the night. In the dark shadows, we swayed alone as my heart raced until it felt as though it would burst out of my chest. This was definitely a burning in my bosom of another kind. It was the most romantic moment of my eleven years of life. I had tasted an intimacy that was tantalizing.

Finn and I eventually pulled back from one another and smiled. My first kiss. This burning in the bosom moment rocked my little world. This was not like the burning I had experienced in church. It was more intense and tingled throughout my body. I knew kissing Finn Price was not of the Spirit and felt like it made me unworthy of the Spirit's presence and burning. Part of me was passionate about living righteously, and then there was this other part of me that seemed to pull me in a different direction that I had learned was unrighteous. I wanted both to "choose the right" and to kiss Finn Price, and I knew the two were mutually exclusive. I felt like I needed to hide this other part of me from my family and church community—the part that wanted to do things in the shadows. I couldn't see where there was a place for the real me—the one who was very alive with divided passions.

The Birthday Party

It was in the fall of my sixth-grade year when I arrived at Vasiliy Lane's front door for her twelfth birthday party. All of my girlfriends were there and the energy was electric. We were locked in for a sleepover. After dinner, dessert, and gifts, we spread out throughout Vasiliy's house to do the things twelve-year-old girls do at slumber parties: talk about boys, play truth or dare, giggle, and tell scary ghost stories.

"Lisa, come into my room and play the Ouija board with us." Vasiliy beckoned me over.

"What's a Ouija board?" I asked.

"You can ask it questions and it'll give you answers. You can ask it anything you want."

She pulled the box down from a tall closet where it had been strategically hidden. She beckoned to the other three of us to come sit on the floor. She opened a box and placed the board covered by the alphabet in the center of our circle as if we were going to play a game of Life. As she brought out a heart-shaped plastic block with a seeing-eye, she said all we had to do was lightly place our fingers on the block. All four of us did so at the same time.

Vasiliy went first to show us how it was done. After she asked her question, the block began moving around the board. We all accused one another of pushing it. I knew I wasn't pushing it and thought one of my friends had to be. How could this happen otherwise?

It was spelling out an answer for Ruth. We were hushed as the block moved around the board. The room felt eerie. We were all only resting our fingertips on the block, and we didn't have enough control to push it around—and still, it moved. One friend after another asked the Ouija board to predict the future. Then, my turn arrived.

"What is my birthday?" I asked.

December 20, 1969, the box spelled out as it slowly moved around the board.

"How is this moving?" I asked again.

"It's a spirit," said Vasiliy.

"What kind of spirit?"

"I don't know…just a spirit."

"Who am I going to marry?" I asked Ouija.

One at a time, the block sat over each letter of Finn Price's name. We all giggled quietly as each one asked who her Prince Charming would be. Suddenly, a loud noise in the attic caused us all to leap. Vasiliy hurriedly threw the Ouija board back in the box and buried it in the top of her closet. We ran out of the room shivering from exhilaration and fear. We decided to play Bloody Mary and freaked ourselves out even more.

I did not have a way to reconcile all of these dark desires with me as well as the way I lived them out. My religion taught me that I was either righteous or unrighteous, good or bad. There was black and there was white. I lived in a dualistic world where there was no room for mystery when it came to personal righteousness and worthiness. I knew playing with the Ouija board was definitely unrighteous; otherwise we would be playing it alongside Candy Land. It was something I needed to do in the shadows. Kissing Finn, too, was something I needed to do in the shadows. It wasn't righteous—and I liked it. But also I wanted to be worthy of Heavenly Father's love and blessings, and these activities clearly made me unworthy and unrighteous. I was convinced I just needed to keep trying harder to be good.

My Bishop's Interview

As I approached my twelfth birthday, excitement in me grew as I anticipated graduating from Primary and entering the Young Women's Organization. In order to graduate into the program, I would need to be able to recite our thirteen Articles of Faith by memory in one of many "worthiness interviews" with my bishop. Our bishop stood in judgment of our personal worthiness. He was also the one who provided a way back to worthiness for those who had fallen from righteous standing due to the commission of certain sins and were seeking a way back to holiness. He "represented the Savior" to our ward members as he fulfilled these roles.[12] My bishop was my mediator between Heavenly Father and me. He was a layperson, the leader of our ward, who had been deemed righteous and worthy to hold the office of bishop. He was the one who would determine whether or not I was worthy to progress.

I labored away in my memory work, preparing for that day when I would be judged. How I desired to be found worthy of promotion! I knew I needed to keep my shadow-side in the dark—the part of me that liked kissing Finn, secretly read *Forever* with friends at school (a sex education I wouldn't wish upon any young child), and played with a Ouija board. I was only twelve and struggling with desires and behaviors that made me feel unrighteous and think that I was unworthy of Heavenly Father's love and acceptance. I felt like I was in a dance, where part of me moved in the light—the part of me that desired and strove to live righteously. The other side of me, my shadow side, moved to another rhythm. I felt the tension of competing impulses—hiding and being seen—always pulling against each other. If I kept performing, kept winning, kept checking off all of the religious boxes, perhaps I could keep my dark side disguised. As long as I kept performing, I would remain safe and appear worthy. But I knew my performance would not secure unconditional love and acceptance, for I was the keeper of the secrets I kept hidden in the shadows, and Heavenly Father knew them all.

I sat across the desk from my bishop in his office, my nerves causing me to jitter. I had run through these tenets of my religion over and over in my mind. The thirteenth Article of Faith was the one that made me the most nervous because of its long list of character traits I needed to recite in the right order. My insides jittered and my palms were clammy. After answering some questions from my bishop about my faith and virtue—and successfully hiding the unvirtuous parts of me—it was time to begin rattling off our basic doctrines and practices from memory:

1. We believe in God, the Eternal Father; and in his Son, Jesus Christ; and in the Holy Ghost.

2. We believe that men will be punished for their own sins, and not for Adam's transgression.

3. We believe that through the Atonement of Christ, all mankind may be saved, by obedience to the laws and ordinances of the Gospel.

4. We believe that the first principles and ordinances of the Gospel are: first, faith in the Lord Jesus Christ; second, repentance; third, baptism by immersion for the remission of sins; fourth, laying on of hands for the gift of the Holy Ghost.

5. We believe that a man must be called of God, by prophecy and by the laying on of hands by those who are in authority, to preach the Gospel and administer in the ordinances thereof.

6. We believe in the same organization that existed in the Primitive Church, namely, apostles, prophets, pastors, teachers, evangelists, and so forth.

7. We believe in the gift of tongues, prophecy, revelation, visions, healing (the laying on of hands for priesthood blessing), interpretation of tongues, and so forth.

8. We believe the Bible to be the word of God as far as it is translated correctly; we also believe the Book of Mormon to be the word of God.

9. We believe all that God has revealed, all that he does now reveal, and we believe that he will yet reveal many great and important things pertaining to the Kingdom of God.

10. We believe in the literal gathering of Israel and in the restoration of the Ten Tribes; that Zion (the New Jerusalem) will be built upon the American continent; that Christ will reign personally upon the earth; and that the earth will be renewed and receive its paradisiacal glory.

11. We claim the privilege of worshiping Almighty God according to the dictates of our own conscience, and allow all men the same privilege, let them worship how, where, or what they may.

12. We believe in being subject to kings, presidents, rulers, and magistrates, in obeying, honoring, and sustaining the law.

13. We believe in being honest, true, chaste, benevolent, virtuous, and in doing good to all men; indeed, we may say that we follow the admonition of Paul—we believe all things, we hope all things, we have endured many things, and hope to be able to endure all things. If there is anything virtuous, lovely, or of good report or praiseworthy, we seek after these things.

Despite my nerves and my jumping insides, I recited the Articles of Faith perfectly. I shook the bishop's hand and he gave me a hug. I exited his office filled with relief, all the while knowing that my personal worthiness was the hinge on which my relationship to God swung. And not only that—my exaltation to godhood was dependent upon it. It was up to me to make myself worthy of the Spirit's presence and Heavenly Father's help, and my worthiness was based on my choices and actions. I hungered to be worthy. I hungered to be good enough. If I obeyed the commandments and lived righteously, if I made myself worthy of His presence, Heavenly Father would draw near to me.

From Pebbles to Boulders

When we think we can win God's approval through our
moral performance and obedience becomes a crushing
burden, then we are "under law." But when we learn that
Christ has fulfilled the law for us and that now we who believe
in him are secure in God's love, then we naturally want to
delight, resemble, and know the One who has done this.[1]

TIM KELLER

I pulled on my ruffled sweater, skirt, and tights. I finished off my
outfit with my first pair of pumps, garnished with a clip-on bow,
as I readied myself for my first Sunday as a Beehive, the designation
given to those who join the entry-level class for girls twelve to eighteen years-old in the Church's Young Women's Organization. I curled
my pin-straight hair until it had my desired flip, ate breakfast, and
jumped into our minivan with the rest of the family for the one-block
drive to church. It was the dead of winter in Salt Lake City, and not
walking weather.

I so longed to be a teenager and was ready to graduate from Primary. I was five feet six inches tall and wearing a training bra while sitting in the Primary with kids half my height. Pounding my fist against
the palm of my receiving hand while singing "Book of Mormon

Stories" didn't hold the same appeal as it had when I was six. I ached to grow up and experience all that the next season of life would bring. Graduating from Primary was a significant move toward the coveted state of teenage bliss.

I joined all the Young Women for an opening hymn and prayer before we dispersed into three classes. I felt young as I looked around—some of these girls were almost to an age where they could be married.

My own class, though, was filled with twelve- and thirteen-year-olds. The Beehive class was about strengthening my faith in Heavenly Father and Jesus Christ and learning to work with others in harmony and cooperation. It was a time for me to grow strong, to stand for truth and righteousness, and to "arise and shine forth."[2]

We all sat around in a circle in folding chairs as I was welcomed into the class. I was introduced to the Young Women's motto as the girls and our teacher stood and recited it together:

> We are daughters of our Heavenly Father, who loves us, and we love him. We will stand as witnesses of God at all times and in all things and in all places as we strive to live the Young Women values, which are faith, divine nature, individual worth, knowledge, choice and accountability, good works, integrity, and virtue. We believe as we come to accept and act upon these values, we will be prepared to strengthen home and family, make and keep sacred covenants, receive the ordinances of the Temple, and enjoy the blessings of exaltation.

Every week we recited the motto, committing it to memory. Our lesson topics included the basics of our faith: who our God is, who we are, our plan of salvation, the apostasy of the Christian church, and restoration of the gospel through the Mormon Church, prophets and revelation, Temple marriage and ordinances, and more. The constant repetition embedded the Mormon doctrines deep into my mind.

One of the most awkward lessons I remember was a class on the Law of Chastity. The class was taught by Sister Young, who looked us in the eyes with the deepest sincerity and said, "Decide today how far you will let boys go with you when you begin dating. Then, you will always be able to confidently draw the line in the sand and won't compromise your virtue in the moment." Just weeks before I had been pounding my hands together, belting out Book of Mormon stories in Primary. Welcome to being an almost-teen!

Sister Young drew a vertical line on the board and wrote, from top to bottom, *kissing, necking, necking and petting, heavy petting, intercourse.* It was the slippery slope to sexual sin, all mapped out for us. A few of us giggled. These were not topics we discussed with any adults—not even our parents.

Sister Young asked us to define each of the terms she'd written. I squirmed in my pumps, wool skirt, and sweater. The line on the board made clear the line I would have to draw to remain virtuous. Mormonism excelled at teaching us the black-and-white nature of the laws and ordinances of the gospel. From that day forward, it was crystal clear to me what I needed to resist in order to be virtuous. And it was crystal clear that I had already compromised my virtue somewhat because I kissed Finn at such a young age.

Sister Young asked us to commit to remain virtuous so that we could marry in the Temple one day. I wanted that with all my heart and wouldn't compromise that dream. And, according to Mormon Scripture, sexual sins are "the most abominable of all sins, save it be the shedding of innocent blood or denying the Holy Ghost."[3] I couldn't imagine how I could ever live with myself if I committed a sin on par with murder or denying the Holy Ghost. The consequences would be unbearable in every way—spiritually, physically, and socially. I would preserve myself for marriage, which I was sure would happen within the next decade. Almost all Mormon girls in Utah were married by the time they finished college.

Dunkings for the Deceased

As a Beehive, I was finally old enough to participate in our Temple ordinance called "baptisms for the dead." I had heard about this practice all my life, but always as a youth activity reserved for older kids—and I was finally one of the older kids. I believed that a critical step toward one day qualifying to receive eternal life was to have a Mormon water baptism by immersion. Those who lived and passed away before Joseph Smith established the Mormon Church needed the opportunity to be baptized as a Mormon. Also, friends and family members who never had the opportunity to receive a Mormon baptism on this earth would have the opportunity to do so in a place between heaven and earth. After they died, they went to a spirit world in which they would have the opportunity to accept or reject the baptism done for them by proxy, often by Mormon youth.

It was my turn to do Temple work. I was privileged to stand proxy for people who were powerless to move on in exaltation without my opening that door for them. It was a pretty amazing power for a twelve-year-old girl. First, I needed to be interviewed by my bishop to determine if I was worthy to be given a temporary Temple "recommend." I just needed to give all the right answers. It would be horrible to be the one girl found "not worthy" to join my class on their first trip to the Temple.

I passed the test and was found worthy for this special youth activity. With Temple recommends in hand and dressed in our Sunday best, the Beehives and the Aaronic priests loaded into several vehicles with our leaders and made the twelve-minute trip downtown to the Salt Lake Temple.

As we walked into the Temple lobby, one by one we flashed our Temple recommends to the Temple worker at the entrance and were escorted to a stairwell to the basement. Somehow, I ended up being separated from my group and I wandered down a hall looking for them. I looked into several large rooms before a worker intercepted me. I did not know I was not supposed to be on that floor, and I felt a little heroic that I had mistakenly seen a few rooms of the Temple that were off limits to me. My mind began to wonder about what went on in those rooms. The Temple ceremony was a massive secret held only by Temple-worthy adults in the church.

As I rejoined my friends, we were escorted down the stairwell and into a large waiting room. The boys went into one changing room and the girls into another, where we were given our baptismal garments. As I changed into the white baptismal gown, my own baptism four years earlier came to mind. Though I felt less innocent at twelve than I had at eight, I still hungered for Heavenly Father's acceptance and love. I still yearned to please Him.

After donning our white clothes, we were reintroduced to the young priests and seated on big, comfy benches where we awaited our turn for proxy baptism. We were in a large room with a beautiful white baptismal font that rested on twelve gold-leaf-covered rams. It was a massive creation. This was as close to the holy of holies (the Celestial Room) as I was going to get until I married in the Temple, so I felt like I was standing on holy ground. We all sat reverently in line, awaiting the mysterious journey ahead. In the Temple, we were asked to be quiet, for it was a holy and peaceful place. So, there I sat with my group of about fifteen preteens, waiting to perform our great act of righteousness.

When my turn arrived, I was beckoned to enter the font by a man who was standing waist-deep in water. As I walked up the stairs of the font, there was a man sitting on a platform observing every baptism to make sure each one was done properly. This meant the baptizer needed to say each word of the baptism mantra correctly, and the person being baptized had to be completely submerged under water. I stepped down. The warm water rose to my waist.

As my baptizer began, I was transported back to my own baptism—but I wasn't in my dad's arms and this time I felt like I was simply going through the motions. Unlike before, the onlookers weren't my mom and siblings, grandparents, and cousins, but other twelve-year-old kids waiting their turns. The other big difference was that, while I had understood every word of my own baptism, I couldn't decipher what my baptizer was saying as he launched into the mantra. He spoke so quickly that I had no clue what he was saying. There were two small screens just outside the font; both were at the eye level of the baptizer. One of them contained the script, and the second flashed names of the deceased people needing my baptism. And then—bam—I was plunged backwards into the lukewarm water.

I was caught off guard by the timing because of my inability to decipher his words, which meant that I couldn't even plug my nose in time. As he brought me out of the water, he began the process again. After several such dunkings, I realized he was speaking so quickly because we had so many people to baptize. "In the name of the Father, the Son and the Holy Spirit, I baptize you, [some unknown dead person's name]." And then came the backwards dunk. Over and over and over. He was talking so quickly that it sounded like my baptizer was speaking a foreign language. And then I realized the names he stated *were* foreign. I didn't have time to wipe my eyes in between dunks. I just kept them squeezed tightly shut and kept one hand over my nose to plug it each time I was immersed. Over and over and over I went under and came up out of the water.

I felt a little waterlogged as we finished. I wiped my eyes dry and climbed the few stairs to exit the font. This all felt strange—but at the same time, I was proud to be a part of Heavenly Father's work on earth. I returned to the dressing room, changed into my Sunday best, and waited for my classmates to complete their baptisms.

Baptisms for the dead were one reason we took genealogy so seriously. We believed we held the responsibility to ensure that all past family members and people who lived on the earth before the founding of the Mormon Church were given an opportunity to accept or reject a Mormon baptism and Temple ordinances. Without them, the Celestial Kingdom would be unattainable for these billions of people—meaning no eternal life in the presence of Heavenly Father and Jesus Christ, no exaltation into godhood. As a result, Mormons are passionate about ensuring that every person who has lived on this earth has the opportunity to accept a Mormon baptism after they die and reside in a transitional place between earth and heaven.

A Child Is Born

The highlight of my twelfth year of life was the birth of my little brother, Matt. I had a brother three years older than me and a sister two years younger. My parents had always desired to have more children. But for a ten-year period after my sister was born, my mom had endured many complications that prevented her from successful pregnancies. This was an excruciating loss for my parents, as they ached to have more children. They said they would have brought ten spirits into this world had they been able. And then came Matt—a supernatural wonder. My mom had "felt inspired" that there were more children in the preexisting world who were part of our family and she and my dad wanted to get them to earth so they could continue their journey in our Great Plan of Happiness.

When Matt arrived on this earth, he brought me pure joy. I quickly assumed the role of nanny. Two years later my mom gave birth to my youngest sister, who doubled my delight. Family was everything to us, and the expansion of our family was a blessing. Mormon families couldn't have too many children—the more the better. Some of my friends had nine or even eleven siblings, which seemed like a party waiting to happen. Because we believed families were eternal, the more children one had, the larger one's kingdom in the afterlife would be. I could not wait until I was a mom and could enjoy the ultimate fulfillment for which I was designed. The Young Women's Organization would help prepare me for that life calling.

When I entered the Young Women's Organization, I was introduced to the Personal Progress program, which centered on homemaking activities and spiritual training in six areas of focus. There were lessons for each value, culminating in an intensive project. These lessons were intended to help me form habits that would make me more Christlike.

Between our Sunday lessons, mid-week youth gatherings, and these programs, I possessed a clear vision of the life I was to strive to live that would help me become more Christlike, prepare me to be married in the Temple, and mature me into a successful home-maker. The Personal Progress program required I complete over seventy hours of service and Scripture study in order to be awarded my medallion. Every Mormon girl wants the gorgeous ruby-adorned medallion imprinted with the Temple to wear around her neck. This all needed to happen amidst my fourteen-plus hours of athletic, dance, and piano commitments each week, as well as my academics.

Striving Toward Perfection

At twelve years old, I was at tennis lessons by six o'clock in the morning several days per week. On the off days, I was up practicing piano for an hour before school began because, after school, my mom picked up my sister and me, brought me a change of clothes, and whisked me off to lessons for the next two to three hours. I had competed in gymnastics, swimming, soccer, diving, and tennis for years. I began taking piano lessons at the age of six, alongside dance lessons. I loved my schedule and participating in all of these activities. In my family, we were always being encouraged toward excellence and perfection. I was blessed with a good deal of athletic ability, enabling me to excel in almost everything I practiced. On top of the hours of extra-curricular activities I participated in was the importance of excelling academically. I was a born perfectionist and our religious and family culture nourished this within me. I put my whole heart into everything I did. In every endeavor, I was determined to excel.

I was taught that Heavenly Father gave me my talents and developing them was part of my divine nature and destiny. Grant Von Harrison captures this idea:

> As premortal spirits, we were responsible for the development of our own abilities, but our individual initiative determined to what degree we took advantage of those opportunities. Our innate abilities at birth are based on the abilities we developed as premortal spirits…in this life, we are primarily responsible for the development of our abilities.[4]

Gaining a mortal body by coming to this earth brought me the opportunity to expand on the progress I had made in developing my talents and abilities in the premortal world. I was blessed with a mom who would pull out every stop to enable me to develop my talents and a dad who was able to provide the resources for me to live this kind of life. Competitive to the core, I took advantage of every opportunity and gave all I could possibly give to grow and succeed. My personality, our religion, and our family culture fueled my passion to win and succeed. The way I strove to make myself worthy of Heavenly Father's presence spilled over into every aspect of my life. Hungry for love and acceptance, I sought to better myself however I possibly could.

There was a tension in all my striving, though. I was encouraged to use my abilities for the Lord's glory—my life was to be lived for Him. On the other hand, I was to live my life for my own glory. Developing my talents would help me in my exaltation into godhood.

Personal Worthiness

Personal worthiness was at the center of my religion. The Young Women's Organization equipped me to identify clearly which actions would increase my worthiness and which would make me unworthy. The end goal of worthiness was a Temple marriage. All my obedience and effort would be for that highest good.

As a child, I was aware there were standards required of me to be worthy, but it didn't feel that weighty because I was young and not as much was required as would be when I grew older. But as I entered my teenage years, what had once felt like laying pebbles into a foundation of eternal life felt more like carrying boulders. It wasn't necessarily the individual acts themselves that felt so weighty. Rather, it was the whole of them and the constant threat of not being worthy that loomed around the corner in the shadows. In addition, the potential of being "found out"—that is, deemed to be unworthy—was daunting and made me anxious. Being human, that was bound to happen.

As a young woman, I was determined to make myself worthy for a Temple marriage one day. I would strive to make that happen, because as far I was concerned, Temple marriage was my only option. If I didn't marry in the Temple, I would forfeit my opportunity for exaltation into goddesshood and would be destined to be a ministering angel to those who have exalted into godhood. Prophet Spencer W. Kimball described the Mormon position on those who do not marry in the Temple:

> No one who rejects the covenant of celestial marriage can reach exaltation in the eternal kingdom of God…No one! It matters not how righteous they may have been, how intelligent or how well trained they are. No one will enter this highest glory unless he enters into the covenant, and this means the new and everlasting covenant of marriage.[5]

Everything in the Young Women's Organization was designed to help prepare me to be worthy of celestial marriage. As much as I longed for that, I also longed for God's blessings. Those blessings came only through obedience. I was taught many formulas, so to speak, for obtaining blessings. If blessings were dispensed according to my good works and obedience, then on the flip side of the coin, those who weren't obedient weren't worthy of blessing. The costs of unworthiness were great. Besides forfeiting Heavenly Father's blessings and presence, shame would be a companion for the unworthy.

The doctrine of conditions-based blessing permeated Mormon life and culture. After all, the object we worship rubs off on us. We were a community of tremendously hard-working people who genuinely desired to serve and bless others by living Christlike lives. My parents were zealous about our religion and actively served their congregations, neighbors, and community. My dad read his Scriptures daily, studying them with fervor. He was faithful in his callings and church attendance and is to this day. Members of our church community took care of each other as well. We took meals to people in need and church members provided for us when we had needs. We baked treats for all our neighbors during the Christmas season and sang carols when we delivered them. Our kitchen was filled with baked goods from ward members throughout the month of December.

I thought every community in America enjoyed this kind of care. When I left the Mormon Church, I expected to experience this kind of community-care everywhere I went. I quickly realized that Mormonism as I knew it provided something unique in its emphasis on care for fellow Mormons. My mom has a heart of mercy so big that she was continually caring for outsiders. From the time I was a teenager, we had people from around the world living in our home. My mom is generous beyond measure, and family is her highest value. She was and is determined to make everyone she meets feel like an insider. I was part of a community of people who were passionate about our religion and living it out during the week, who supported each other faithfully in times of need through acts of service, who were faithful to church callings and sought to live a life worthy of the Spirit's presence and Heavenly Father's blessings, and who were hungry for spiritual experiences.

I survived middle school with the usual multitude of emotional scars inflicted by mean girls and guys and was relieved to finally arrive at East High School in Salt Lake City. I only possessed any amount of self-esteem at this point in my life because of my athletic and academic successes. Now that I was fourteen, I had progressed to the MiaMaid class—the Mutual Improvement Association—in the Young Women's Organization. Love, faith, and purity were emphasized in these years as I pursued the activities on my Personal Progress checklist.

During class on Sunday, and during the midweek activities, we learned the value of male-female relationships and were reminded of the physical boundaries necessary to remain virtuous in those relationships. The sexual purity continuum continued to come up in church lessons. Mormon kids could probably win any speed quiz about the differentiations between petting, heavy petting, and fornication.

The Church teaches that the official age that kids may begin dating is sixteen years old. I had had boyfriends for years by the age of sixteen and didn't feel complete without one. My parents didn't seem to mind my interest in boys and enabled me to hang out with my crushes. Technically I wasn't dating, but I wasn't blocked from nurturing relationships with boys. The dating rule was only binding when I met Jake during my freshman year at East High. His parents were far stricter than mine and held him to the dating law. I could not wait for Jake to turn sixteen.

Church leaders worked to provide opportunities for the youth to socialize in different settings. Among my favorite activities were the "stake youth dances." When I became a MiaMaid, I was finally of age to attend these dances, which were a combination of high school students from multiple stakes (each stake has three wards). In Salt Lake City, where there seemed to be a church house every mile, youth dances were packed and electric. This was especially true on New Year's Eve as the clock struck midnight and kids were strategically sneaking kisses in the church house where "bear hugging" wasn't allowed.

We also had regional and national youth conferences during the summers that we could attend. The church created an environment in which relating with the opposite sex was desirable, and finding the guy I would one day marry was ever on the forefront of my mind—even as a teenager.

The Word of Wisdom

Once I was a high schooler, learning about the Word of Wisdom and morality was central and important given the great temptations teenagers face. The Word of Wisdom is like a Mormon health code. We were to abstain from the consumption of strong drink and wine (alcoholic beverages), hot drinks (coffee and tea), and the use of tobacco.[6] While I was growing up, caffeinated soft drinks were included in the Word of Wisdom's list of things to abstain from because caffeine was associated with "hot drinks." (Today, those soft drinks are perfectly okay to consume for most Mormons.) Obeying the Word of Wisdom was necessary to be worthy of baptism, missionary work, and attending the Temple. Consuming these beverages was sinful and would make me unworthy of the Spirit's presence.

When our family would go out to eat, if wine glasses were present on the table when we were seated, my parents would thrust them away with a bit of disgust. "Would you like to see a drink menu?" the waiter would ask. "We don't drink alcohol," my parents would declare with pride. Their pride and judgment against the evil alcohol could not be contained. The Word of Wisdom made us unique. It definitely set us apart from the rest of the world. Because we lived in Salt Lake City, fifty percent of the population was LDS and adhering to the same Word of Wisdom. I suppose we were not that original in our hometown.

When I arrived at East High, I suddenly found myself amidst a sea of teenagers, many of whom were consuming alcohol. Many of these fellow students who were drinking were Mormons. We called these "rebellious" teens *jack Mormons*. I was determined to stand strong and resist the temptation to break the Word of Wisdom—and the law, for that matter. I developed a fabulous group of friends, most of whom resisted the temptation alongside me during our freshman year of high school. Still, there was something attractive about the freedom the other students seemed to enjoy.

Field Trip

When I was a junior in high school, a young man in our ward was called to be my Sunday School teacher. Brother Maxwell liked field trips. And not field trips of the Mormon kind, but extremely out-of-the-box field trips.

"One of the men hired to wash the windows for my company has invited us to visit his church," he told us one day. "It's called a Pentecostal church."

Whoa. I had never been to another kind of church service. This was wild and crazy for a bunch of Mormon teens.

"I want you to experience a different belief system and way to worship."

We showed up for church the following Sunday wearing our dresses and skirts, suits and ties. The twelve of us piled into a few cars and headed to the new church. Unlike our building, this church was an industrial space with a large room. There were about fifty people filling the chairs that faced a band. Yes, a band. I didn't have a paradigm for these instruments in worship. They were unholy and irreverent. I spent the next eighty minutes in a worship service that boggled my mind and all my categories for proper worship.

A man named John greeted us, his entire face lit up with a smile. He was wearing blue jeans and a white T-shirt. People wore that kind of casual dress to church? *How disrespectful toward Heavenly Father.* A few seconds later, I noticed he had a tattoo crawling up his arm—*sacrilege!* It is wrong to mark one's skin. I was mentally recalculating, struggling to fit all these observations together with the reality that John loved God.

He seated us in a row of chairs along the back wall, so we were set apart from the congregation. The band hit their first chord. While the electric guitarist did his thing and the drummer pounded loudly, the congregation lifted their voices and—this I couldn't believe—*clapped their hands.*

I looked down the row at my friends and we all giggled out our discomfort. Right worship—holy worship—was reverent, quiet, soft-spoken, and solemn. But these rock-band instruments, casual clothing, and clapping...all of this was unholy and inappropriate. We snickered and judged them all the way back to our reverent ward house, for what else would we do with what we had just encountered? We only had black and white categories with which to filter information and experiences. This experience didn't align with ours, so it was wrong. It was crazy.

As I sat snickering alongside my peers, I could not have imagined in my wildest dreams that I would one day find this style of worship like cold water to my thirsty soul. Never could I fathom experiencing God so vividly in that way, not in a million of my wildest dreams.

Breaking Free of Shame's Straitjacket

Moralism is death on spirituality. Moralism is the approach
that puts all the emphasis on our performance. It operates
out of a conviction that there's a clear-cut right that we're
capable of discerning, choosing, and carrying out in
every and all circumstances. It puts the entire burden
of our spirituality on what we do. God is marginalized.
And it crushes our spirits. There's no mercy in it.[1]

EUGENE PETERSON

t this point in my life, all of the requirements for worthiness I was trying to uphold felt like transporting boulders into the bedrock of my eternal life. I dug deep to resist the weekly invitations to consume alcohol from friends and acquaintances who had fallen into its clutches. In my imagination, it seemed like a night of inebriation would release the pressure to perform for a window of time. My drunk friends were abandoned into a world with seemingly fewer cares when under the influence of alcohol. I was hungry to experience both of those things. I also transitioned to an East High boyfriend during my freshman year and was crazy about him. Navigating the deep waters of teenage attraction challenged me to remain virtuous at all times and in all places. We were good kids who wanted to choose the right, but we were also drawn to the shadows, where temptations that made us unrighteous and unworthy beckoned us.

One of the support systems the Church has in place to educate its teens during the high school years is called "seminary." In Utah, I was able to take my seminary class as one of my class periods in my school schedule. The Church conveniently owned a building across the street from the school, in which hundreds of students gathered throughout the day. Seminary teachers are married men who have chosen that work as their vocation and are employees of the LDS Church. They are usually passionate about youth and the gospel they teach.

In the middle of my junior year at East High I plopped down at my desk in the seminary building. Mr. Peterberg began our lesson as he did every day. Somewhere in that fifty-minute period, I was confronted with one of the most jarring stories of my faith I had ever heard. As if he was talking about going to the dentist for a checkup, Mr. Peterberg taught us that Jesus was conceived by Heavenly Father, who was flesh and bones, by having intercourse with Mary.[2]

If I had ever heard this doctrine before, it had blown right past me. I was horrified by this revelation. Heavenly Father had a wife! I had also believed that Mary had conceived Jesus by the Holy Spirit. You know, the virgin birth idea. So, not only would my God have committed adultery but incest as well. (This would be incest because Mary was literally conceived by Heavenly Father and Heavenly Mother in the preexisting world, so she was their daughter. This doctrine would have them having intercourse with one another.)

"What!" I exclaimed. "Will you say that again?!"

Mr. Peterberg explained the story once more. "The Holy Ghost empowered Mary to live in the presence of Heavenly Father and made her worthy of His physically impregnating her. If Mary was overcome only by the Holy Spirit, then Jesus wouldn't be the 'only begotten Son' of God on this earth. Because we believe the Holy Ghost is not God the Father but another god, Jesus would be the son of the Holy Spirit if the Father didn't overcome her and physically impregnate her."

Again, I had no category into which to place this piece of doctrine and was deeply disturbed. "That's disgusting! That's incest!" I exclaimed. There were some other murmurings around the classroom. As I sought to make sense of this jarring revelation, I asked more questions. Our conversation ended abruptly when Mr. Peterberg said, "There are some beliefs we hold that don't make sense to us. When we come to these places, we choose to accept them and believe."

I don't remember being jarred by any doctrine I held until this moment in seminary. I had just accepted and believed all that I had been so diligently and genuinely taught. I had learned not to doubt my beliefs. And if I did question, it needed to be with a sincerity to understand and come to acceptance. But this was not sitting well with me. I sat in my chair dumbfounded. Disturbed. Disillusioned. Feeling whiplashed, I made my way across the street for seventh period.

Another such occasion occurred when I was seventeen years old. I was in my second year as a Laurel in the Young Women's Organization. The purpose of the Laurel class, which consisted of sixteen and seventeen-year-old girls, was to prepare us to make and keep sacred covenants and receive the Temple ordinances. There was a lot of teaching about the importance of sexual purity, remaining virtuous, and making ourselves worthy to marry in the Temple one day—hopefully in the not-too-distant future. Throughout my life in the Young Women's program, I was thoroughly educated about the boundary lines between righteous and unrighteous living. Our church leaders expertly taught us the essential doctrines of our faith. One of the teachings that was difficult for me to swallow was that the Mormon's practice of polygamy had been only temporarily suspended, not banished altogether. There was a strong possibility that, when I arrived in the Celestial Kingdom, I would be a polygamous wife and would give birth to spirit children throughout eternity. My earthly husband would be a god, and the other wives and I would birth his spirit children and populate his kingdom.[3] This was the end reward of all my effort to be worthy of a Temple marriage. Just the idea of it felt repulsive and minimizing to me.

One afternoon, I approached my mom and asked her, "What do you think about being a polygamous wife throughout eternity? How do you deal with that?" I genuinely desired to know, because I wasn't dealing with it well. She responded, "I choose not to think about that, Lisa. I just can't think about it."

I understood completely and felt empathy toward my mom. At the same time, I was bewildered. How could she not think about her eternal destiny? This was my future in eternal glory and I could not imagine how I would survive it. I repeated to myself what I had been told—*I'll be perfect then, and in my perfection, it won't bother me. Heavenly Father's plan is perfect and so it will make sense when I'm in heaven.* But it bothered me now and it was impossible to imagine it not bothering me in the Celestial Kingdom. I had chosen not to think about it for years. But as I grew closer to a marrying age, I needed to wrestle with the reality that polygamy was very possibly my future as a Mormon goddess.

My mother's response reinforced the concept that had been instilled in me and that I had experienced throughout my life: *Don't question. Don't wrestle with the sticky beliefs. We can't intellectualize faith.* In fact, I sensed a spirit of judgment from leaders toward those who sought to reason with their beliefs. It was not learning that was looked down upon, rather questioning with skepticism.

My freshman through junior years of high school were filled with academics, hours of tennis practice and tournaments, a boyfriend, and a friend group. I was sidelined from tennis my junior year because of severe back injuries, which was painful and frustrating. My mom pulled out all the stops to find the therapists, sports psychologists, and medical care that would enable me to return to the court. After much therapy and rehab, I returned to the court my senior year with a back brace and muscle relaxers.

By this time, more and more of my friends had experimented with alcohol, and on most weekends resisting the temptation to join them required a fierce internal battle. But my desire to be virtuous was stronger. Constantly before me were reminders of what it takes to merit the Spirit's presence:

> Virtuous living "at all times and in all things, and in all
> places" qualifies you for the constant companionship of
> the Holy Ghost…Since the Holy Ghost does not dwell in
> unclean tabernacles, living a virtuous life is a prerequisite to
> having the companionship of the Holy Ghost and receiv-
> ing the blessings of Temple ordinances.[4]

"At all times and in all things, and in all places" was the standard of qualification for the Holy Ghost's companionship. I felt that pressure so much of the time. It felt like a weight on my shoulders that I carried with me everywhere; it felt like a standard against which I had fallen ridiculously short. The Holy Ghost did not dwell in unclean tabernacles, of this I was sure. Making myself clean and righteous enough to qualify me for the companionship of the Holy Ghost reminded me of the spiritual boulders I was dragging around during this season of my life. No longer was a weekly trip to church all I needed to do to make myself worthy. There were innumerable decisions I needed to make all day long: resist cussing and sexual impurity, keep the Word of Wisdom, pay a full tithe, attend church faithfully, participate in youth activities, and keep my mind and speech clean. There were teenagers around me who seemed to be successfully attaining the status of "possessing a clean tabernacle." Why was it so hard for me? I felt unworthy and covered in shame. I attended church with my family every Sunday but was growing weary of the conditional love and acceptance that accompanied our moralistic doctrine and filtered into our family culture.

The Mormon law was crushing my spirit. I longed to be completely seen and found worthy of love with all of my imperfections. On top of the general pressure of the law, certain sins required an appointment with my bishop, during which I would confess my sins with the intent of repenting and no longer committing the sins. The thought of sitting across from my bishop in his office behind a closed door, looking into his face, and sharing my deep, dark secret sins with him felt about as natural to me as breathing under water. I was very aware of my lack of resolve to overcome and stop the practice of these sins. Because I wasn't ready to repent and stop committing these transgressions, I decided it was useless to confess to my bishop. Why bother if I didn't have a will to repent?

I was taught that there are varying degrees of sin, some much graver than others. I did not have to confess the lighter-weight sins to my bishop. The bishop would also determine my level of personal worthiness based on my contriteness of heart over my sins committed, as well as whether I would need consequences, like abstaining from partaking of the sacrament during Sunday services. The thought was dreadful. Everyone in the service knew what it meant when someone was not worthy to partake of the sacrament. For me, it would have meant being on the fast track to social shame. On many Sundays, I had been guilty myself of looking around curiously to see if anyone was abstaining from partaking of the bread and water as it was passed throughout the congregation. I didn't want to be one of them.

My internal shame felt like a wet blanket covering me, and adding public humiliation to the mix was a dreaded thought. I couldn't do that. I could not have articulated that I was longing to be loved and accepted in spite of myself. I needed to keep the real me hidden and disguised, for I was not acceptable as I was. The eight-year-old me who proudly wore her CTR ring and desired to live righteously was still very present within me, creating tension with seventeen-year-old me, who was looking for unconditional love and acceptance in spaces I shouldn't have. I could not see a way to align all the voices within me.

My desire to experience freedom from the demands of my religion grew stronger with each passing week. I wasn't living as virtuously as I should have been and didn't feel like I had the capacity to do so at the time. There were sins I was committing that required visiting my bishop for a time of confession, but these sins also provided me an opportunity to feel loved and accepted outside of the requirement for moral performance. I was attracted to a different kind of life than the one I was living—one that tasted freedom. Partying and rebellion was the only path in which I could envision tasting freedom. To confess this to my bishop would have only plunged me deeper into the pool of shame in which I had been swimming for years.

This attraction to freedom throughout my high school years created tension in my relationship with my parents. I didn't feel free to share the stirrings within me, my attraction to particular temptations, and my failure to live righteously. I think this was partly because of the influence of our beliefs and the Mormon culture in which we lived and breathed every day of our lives. There wasn't space in our relationship for this kind of wrestling. It was also partly because I was their daughter and there are many things that would have been utterly awkward to share with them, simply because they were my parents. They believed with all their hearts that this faithful Mormon life was the path to happiness and they wanted that for me. They were parenting the best they knew how and I was navigating my teenage years the best I knew how. The tension between our bests worked hard to pull us apart. Thankfully, one of my sisters had become one of my closest friends, which was a gift throughout those years as well as our adult lives. I drew comfort from knowing that I could mostly be myself with one family member.

> I couldn't see a way to align all the voices within me.

The Pendulum Swings

As summer came to an end, my senior year was fast approaching. My friends were all attending an end-of-summer party at a friend's giant condominium in Park City. I was ready to put off the Word of Wisdom fully and plunge into a year of experimentation. I could taste the freedom awaiting me, and I was eagerly awaiting the night ahead as my friends and I drove up the canyon that afternoon. When I walked through the door, my classmates were completely shocked that I was there and they welcomed me with open arms. There were dropped-jaws and cheers from a few who had never seen me at one of these events. It felt good to be so warmly received by this crowd.

It took the plunge into the party scene with gusto. I drank my first beer—swallowing quickly to get the nasty taste out of my mouth. Then I was introduced to a beer bong and realized I could guzzle several beers down in seconds, bringing on an altered state much more swiftly. Oh, the wonders of the underworld.

My first "buzz" arrived, releasing me from the confines of self-awareness. All the cares in the world drifted away. Before much time had passed, I was drunk and one with the crowd. All of my inhibitions had dissipated, and I was enjoying a state of being I had never encountered before. No pressures. No need to perform. People with whom I hardly ever conversed suddenly felt like family. And the cares of the world were gone. All that was required to experience these pleasures was the consumption of alcohol. As the night progressed, I laughed hard and celebrated freedom without restraint. I noticed some people weren't holding their alcohol and were hanging over toilets, losing their lunch and dinner. That would have been awful. But that never happened to me. It was just a night filled with a freedom that I had resisted for three long years of high school, and I desired more.

> I was enjoying a state of being I had never encountered before. No pressures. No performances.

My life's pendulum swung from legalism (acceptance based on performance) to licentiousness (lacking moral restraint and a disregard for rules). Partying was the only thing I could find to experience freedom from the pressure of the Mormon system of personal righteousness and worthiness. Though I could not articulate it at the time, I desperately longed to be loved and accepted without conditions—for the *real me,* with all my light and darkness, to be embraced. I ached to be released from the shame created by a culture of striving for personal worthiness, sometimes succeeding and sometimes failing.

Tennis and academics consumed my weekdays and parties greeted me on weekends. I shut down my conscience one choice at a time, one party at a time. I had to do that in order to plunge into the party world without cognitive dissonance. I lived from party to party, hungry for the next weekend when the cares of the world would dissipate into the stream of alcohol working its way through my body. For a short time, I managed to keep my choice to party hidden from my parents. But only for a short time.

It was the end of September and East High's homecoming weekend was swiftly approaching. Unlike all of the previous three years' formal events I had attended, the planning for this formal was a bit more involved for my friends and me with the presence of alcohol. We needed to navigate how to stealthily obtain illegal substances as well as find a place to safely consume them following the school events. My friends who had been partying for longer than a few months figured out all the details, and I went along for the ride.

My date rang the doorbell of our lovely red brick colonial home, nicely accented by black shutters. After my parents snapped a few pictures of us—Jude, in his suit, and me in my red dress and pumps with my hair curled and bangs teased—we climbed into his little hatchback and excitedly sped off to meet a group of friends downtown for dinner. As I climbed into the car, I noticed that Jude had acquired a fifth of Crown Royal whiskey as well as some Peach Schnapps and vodka. I was quickly being introduced to all of the mixers that made a glass of alcohol go down as smoothly as possible, as well as the drinks we could manage to sneak into a glass of Sprite or Coca-Cola at a restaurant. I was swiftly learning that the high school party world had a well-developed subculture.

Throughout dinner we each consumed a mini-bottle or two of Schnapps, nothing significant enough to bring on a buzz, yet enough to make us feel like we were cool. The real party would begin right after the school dance concluded. My friends had a reserved a hotel room upstairs from the dance for the night. This would make for a smooth transition to the after-party.

As Jude and I were driving from the restaurant to our homecoming dance, red lights began flashing from behind us. My heart began to race as a police officer approached our car. Jude reclined his chair significantly to mask the alcohol on the floor behind the seat. I thought that would be a dead giveaway to the officer. Jude rolled down his window and greeted the officer. Evidently, he had rolled through a stop sign. After some conversation and shining his flashlight around the car, the officer gave Jude a warning and sent us on our way. My heart felt like it was going to burst out of my chest. I exhaled five minutes' worth of breath as we rolled away. I had no idea this would be a foreshadowing of events to come.

We made our entrance into the University Park Hotel, posed for pictures to capture this historic day, and headed into the dance. Jude eventually disappeared while I danced with friends in a mob. After an hour, I was greeted by our vice-principal, who was strict and kept his standards so high that nobody liked him. He asked me to follow him. We wandered down a stairwell into the bowels of the building and landed in a small room. I was clueless as to why I was there. Mr. Trillo asked me if I had been drinking. I told him I hadn't consumed alcohol at the dance, but had drunk a mini-bottle at dinner before arriving at the school function. He worked to get me to confess to drinking at the school function, but it wasn't true, and I was sober to prove it. As one thing led to another, he told me that Jude had been caught bringing the Crown Royal into the hotel, and I was guilty by association because I was his date. I told Mr. Trillo that I hadn't seen Jude since we arrived. He didn't care. As he picked up the phone to call my parents, I asked him if I could please be the bearer of bad news. I felt like I had been punched in the gut, and I dreaded this call.

My dad arrived at the hotel and looked concerned. He was serious, but he wasn't as angry as I thought he might be. He also sided with me about the injustice of the situation. This was my first offense and I had made a good case for my innocence. Two days later, my parents and I sat across from Mr. Trillo in his East High office while he shared that I would be suspended from school for the week and suspended from my student body office until January.

The meeting was surreal. For so much of my life, I had desperately worked to choose the right, to please, to evade my shame with academic and athletic successes, and to faithfully live the commandments. And now I was the one being *suspended*. The high-achieving student, athlete, and student-body officer—suspended. Had I not hungered so desperately for freedom, this might have been a wake-up call. What I could not see at the time was that in my pursuit of freedom from shame and search for acceptance outside of my performance, my soul was becoming tangled in an even deeper bondage.

As I continued to indulge in licentious behavior, I walked through doors I would never have considered opening previously. Thankfully, I hadn't lost all sense or wisdom. I knew this would be only a season of my life—a short season in the scheme of my entire life. I had seen

> In my search for acceptance outside of my performance, my soul was becoming tangled in an even deeper bondage.

so many fellow Mormons take this path. In Salt Lake City, risky behavior was quite common. I knew that one day I would "clean up my act" and marry in the Temple. This rebellious season might last a few years, and then I would return to a life of working to obey the commandments of Mormonism and prepare myself to be worthy of participating in Temple covenants. Until then, I was enjoying my freedom.

After my parents busted me several more times with alcohol on my breath following the homecoming dance, they grew increasingly worried. My mom did her best to come toward me in my moments of inebriation, asking me *why* I was drinking alcohol and *when* I would stop. My dad struggled with so much anger about my rebellion that he chose not to engage with me. It was challenging for him to hold back his shame and judgment of me, which tended to seep out slowly. I was no longer choosing the right and it was emotionally costly for us all. Unlike my parents, I had the next party to help me escape reality. Once I began shutting down my conscience, it became easier to ignore it the next time it popped up for some attention.

Because of the injuries that had sidelined me from tennis during my junior year of high school, I was rehabbing throughout the college recruiting season. I wanted nothing more than to play tennis for a university. The therapies didn't bring much healing or relief from the pain. Despite this, I decided to return to the court just before my senior year, wearing a back brace and armed with muscle relaxers for my post-game pain management. Toward the end of my senior year, I was offered a walk-on spot at Brigham Young University, which was ranked seventh in the nation at the time. I was elated that I would be playing college tennis if I accepted that offer, but I wasn't terribly excited to live in "Happy Valley" (which is what Salt Lakers called Provo, Utah). BYU was ninety-eight percent Mormon and had high moral standards. Because I wasn't abiding by all of these standards and didn't think I was ready to repent yet, this was a drawback for me.

The following is just a taste of BYU's strict honor code:

- no tank tops
- no short shorts
- no alcohol, tobacco, or drugs
- no co-ed dorm visits
- no grubby facial hair for guys
- no backless dresses
- no going braless
- skirts must come to the knees
- piercings for girls only—and only one pair of earrings at a time
- no extreme styles or brightly colored hair
- nothing dirty, frayed, or patched may be worn
- regular attendance in church required—women in dresses and men in ties
- no tattoos exposed

This was only part of the honor code. I didn't fault BYU for their honor code because it represented our church and required students to meet its standards. It would not have crossed my mind to question whether or not it should be in place. My question was whether I was ready to submit myself to it or not.

High school graduation came and went with gusto. I spent the summer at tennis tournaments and parties, drinking my way through weekends. At a national tournament in California, I met the University of Utah coach. Within minutes he had invited me to join the Lady Utes tennis team. The idea of going to college at the University of Utah rather than BYU was liberating. The only drawback was that going to the University of Utah meant living at home for a few more years, since my parents lived two miles from campus. In my naïve view of reality, independence could not come soon enough. I am sure my parents were desiring a bit of independence from the challenges I had brought into their lives as well.

Never in a million years would I have imagined how my life's trajectory would completely reroute only six months from this day. Mr. Peterberg's jarring doctrinal revelation was a foreshadowing of what was in store for me during the next two years of my life. Only God knew that I would spend much of the next two years in a similar state of shock.

Exploring the Web

When you are in the middle of a story it isn't a story at all,
but only a confusion; a dark roaring, a blindness, a wreckage
of shattered glass and splintered wood; like a house in a
whirlwind, or else a boat crushed by the icebergs or swept
over the rapids, and all aboard powerless to stop it. It's
only afterwards that it becomes anything like a story at all.
When you are telling it, to yourself or to someone else.[1]

MARGARET ATWOOD

*O*n a Sunday afternoon in January of 1988, Gary and I sat at his dining table with a Bible study spread before us. It had been six weeks since our disturbing conversation in his car. Though questioning Mormonism so that I could defend it terrified me, a gnawing anxiety had become my constant companion due to my inability to defend my beliefs. I knew they would prove to be true if I studied them more deeply. Studying Mormon doctrine and the Bible would just deepen my testimony of the Mormon Church. This was the only thing that gave me the courage to press into this journey with Gary. I also believed he would come to see the Mormon Church as God's one and only true church on this earth.

The topic of our Bible study was relationships, which seemed romantic and appropriate since we were head over heels for each other. We planned to explore God's design for relationships and how He fit into our relationship. It had never occurred to me that God desired to take up residence in my relationships. Heavenly Father was in relationship with Heavenly Mother on a heavenly planet and seemed distant and disconnected from me and my relationships. I didn't have a paradigm for the idea that God desired to relate with me so personally.

Gary launched into the study. He read through the first page, which talked about God's design for relationships. As we moved through the page I was focused. I assumed I would be familiar with all the concepts we would encounter. I had been thoroughly indoctrinated. But within minutes of beginning the study, I faced the rude awakening that this was not the case. It hit me like a brick wall that I might have been so sheltered in my Mormon community that I didn't have any idea people held such differing views of God.

God Is *What?*

The study began by addressing how the Bible presents God's nature—the Father, the Son, and the Holy Spirit—as one God in a perfect community of love. It talked about how this one God is made up of three persons—the Father, the Son, and the Spirit. This three-in-one God was referred to as the Trinity. I was completely baffled, and we had just begun. There was more confusion to come. As we dug deeper into the nature of the biblical God, the study said that God the Father is spirit. My Mormon God was called Heavenly Father and He was flesh and bones, not spirit.[2] How could God possibly be spirit? That would make Him invisible. I thought everyone believed as Mormons believed that God was flesh and bones. I had no paradigm into which I could fit this view of God, and after strongly reacting, I challenged Gary to show me where the Bible talked about this. Gary read several verses and then landed on John 4:24, "God is spirit, and those who worship him must worship in spirit and truth."

"It really says that in the Bible?" I more stated than asked.

I turned to my King James Version, which read the same. I had always heard this verse through Joseph Smith's translation of the Bible, which puts it differently: "For unto such hath God promised his Spirit. And they who worship him, must worship in spirit and in truth." I thought there must be a way to interpret that verse to show that God is not actually spirit, and that the passage is actually referring to how we are to worship Him. I pushed back.

"There is another way of looking at this." I said. "Heavenly Father isn't invisible. He is flesh and bones like us."

The idea of God as spirit was too far "out there" for me to wrap my mind around. I was confused and, once again, felt as though I was in a doctrinal freefall. But instead of admitting my confusion, I fought this concept of God, sharing my view. Joseph Smith, the beloved founder and first prophet of the Mormon Church, had seen two personages in his first vision after he revised his vision—Heavenly Father and Jesus Christ—who both had physical bodies. So God could not possibly be anything but flesh and bones. I thought everything about this new idea of God was absurd.

Emotions rushed through my body. I argued with Gary, letting him know that it was impossible to comprehend God as a spirit. He shared with me that that is kind of the point. He went on to say that God is completely other: sovereign, all-powerful, all-knowing, incomprehensible to our finite minds. At the same time, he shared that God created us to be in an intimate relationship with Him. I couldn't conceive that God was anything other than like me—flesh and bones. I also couldn't conceive that God wanted to be as intimately involved with me as Gary was claiming. I was skilled in acting and looking religious, which was the extent of my relating to Heavenly Father. This new idea of God was incomprehensible to me.

Gary and I were in combat mode and we had barely started the Bible study. This was going to be a long haul. If I had not been so crazy about Gary, the relationship might have ended along with the conclusion of our first study. But I *was* crazy about him, and the six days in between Bible studies buffered the discomfort of our Sunday study sessions.

Countless conversations about God's nature followed our first one. It felt like Gary and I had opened Pandora's box that winter, and its insides deeply disrupted my interior world. Though I still believed Mormonism was God's true Church, this biblical picture of God created angst in me because it was so different from my picture of God.

After many more debates about whether or not God is spirit, we talked about Jesus, God the Son. As a Mormon, I believed that Jesus is a created being, the first-born begotten son of Heavenly Father and Heavenly Mother in a preexisting world. He is literally the brother of every one of the billions of people who have or who will ever occupy this earth because we were also begotten as spirit intelligences in that preexisting world from the same heavenly parents.

This also meant that Jesus was the brother of Lucifer, for he was the offspring of Heavenly Father and Mother as well. As Heavenly Father was devising His plan for this earth, Jesus proposed that He give people free agency—the ability to choose whether or not they would follow Him. Opposing Jesus, Lucifer proposed that Heavenly Father force people to follow him. This created a war on that planet, each faction fighting for their plan. Lucifer and a third of the host who had followed his plan lost that war and were cast into Outer Darkness, transforming into fallen angels or demons. Jesus and the remaining host who followed His plan remained and now inhabit this earth as part of the Mormon plan of salvation. As a Mormon, I was taught that when Jesus said in John 10:30, "I and the Father are one," He was saying that They are one in purpose. It had never crossed my mind to think of Jesus as God, equal to the Father.

Gary and I continued to spar over the identity of Jesus for months. He introduced me to the Bible passage John 1:1-3 (NIV), "In the beginning was the Word, and the Word was with God, and the Word was God. He was with God in the beginning. Through him all things were made; without him nothing was made that has been made." Because studying the Bible was new to me, I dissected every word of it. Each verse I read led to questions, and then more questions. What was the beginning? Who is the Word? What is the Word? As I investigated, I learned that the Word is Jesus Christ. The Bible teaches that Jesus was with God and He was God.

He was God.

In my average daily conversations, grammar meant what it meant. *Was* meant *was*. However, because my relationships and religious worldview were at stake in this doctrinal search, I engaged in a way of thinking that concluded *was* could not possibly have meant *was*. I challenged the verses and read them over and over, fiercely determined to somehow make sense of this new paradigm and make it consistent with mine.

How could Jesus be God if the Father is God? I argued with Gary over this question for the next eight months. I had always known them to be different gods. There was nothing he could say to help me understand this mystery. It was beyond him and others to do so. As fiercely opposed to the biblical view of God as I was, I began to see that many different beliefs about God existed. But I also believed that, even though people hold different beliefs about God, we are all talking about the same God—we just describe Him differently. I had been taught that even though different religious groups have differing views of God, all views lead to the same God. Muslims call Him Allah, Mormons call Him Heavenly Father, Christians—I had just learned—call Him a Trinity. Whatever attributes were ascribed to Him, I believed everyone was talking about the same God. It wasn't long before Gary challenged this belief as well.

There were many days between Gary's and my doctrinal sparring matches that I had to block out all that I was learning in the Bible. Each new concept seemed to create a new fissure in the Mormon foundation that had supported me for eighteen years of my life.

I had always been taught that knowing spiritual truth came through prayer and receiving a burning in my bosom. I felt like I was cheating on my family and my religion by researching my beliefs and comparing them to biblical doctrine. These feelings made me feel like I was suffocating at times, and I was grateful for the rhythm of school, tennis workouts, and dates with Gary to distract me from the rumblings deep within my soul.

Unchangeable God

My next war with Gary arose when he shared with me the biblical perspectives that God has always been God, and there is only one true God. He said God is unchanging, without beginning or end. Again, a visceral reaction, born out of fear and a sense of absurdity, consumed my body. We proceeded to read many Bible verses indicating God has always been God, all-powerful, all-knowing, perfect, and holy (see Psalm 86:10; Isaiah 43:10-11; Isaiah 46:9; and 1 Timothy 2:5). Isaiah 44:6-8 (NIV) dropped like a bomb onto my fragile foundation:

> This is what the LORD says—
> Israel's King and Redeemer, the LORD Almighty:
> I am the first and I am the last;
> apart from me there is no God....
>
> You are my witnesses. Is there any God besides me?
> No, there is no other Rock; I know not one.

It was difficult to argue with the clarity of these verses. But again my vision was blurry. Each biblical passage I read seemed to thrust me into a wrestling match between what I was reading and what I had always known to be true. I desperately wanted it to remain true. Just the thought of it not being true turned my stomach. The losses would be too great to bear. I attempted to plant my heels into my theology of God, but I was unable to find any proof to defend it biblically. In order to introduce me to the unchanging nature of God, Gary led me to verses like Malachi 3:6, "I the LORD do not change; therefore you, O children of Jacob, are not consumed" and Psalm 90:2, "Before the mountains were brought forth, or ever you had formed the earth and the world, from everlasting to everlasting you are God (ESV)."

Again I attempted to plant my heels into my theology of God's changing nature, but again, I was unable to find any proof to defend it biblically. My Mormon god was once a man who, through his works, exalted into godhood. Like me, he'd once lived on an earth. The Mormon prophet Lorenzo Snow coined a phrase based on Joseph Smith's doctrine of God that my Sunday School teachers taught me as a mantra, "As man now is, God once was. As God now is, man may become."[3] It was deeply ingrained within me that God had once been a finite being and exalted into godhood. I was on this earth to do the same, with the same potential of being exalted into a goddess in heaven if I married in the Mormon Temple and lived a worthy life. I didn't have a paradigm to accommodate this idea of an unchanging God.

In the dead of winter in Salt Lake City, my soul was permeated with the chill of the season. I did not yet embrace this biblical theology of God or the nature of people, yet the reality that the beliefs I held dear did not correlate with the Bible created a fissure that allowed the cold to seep inside of me. The warm comfort of *knowing* the Mormon Church was the true church of God and that Joseph Smith was a true prophet of God was no longer a comforting cloak. Nothing was. I felt exposed and stripped. Each conversation or Bible study with Gary seemed to lead me one step further from comfort and one step closer to isolation.

This was the most excruciating journey of my life up to that point. What made it even more challenging was the reality that I was still living at home with my family. In an ideal world, I would have been able to engage with my parents as I questioned and searched the faith system they knew to be true and held so dear. But Mormonism produced a culture that did not leave room for that. I was haunted by the fear that if I were to come to the decision that Mormonism wasn't true, I would be an apostate. According to Mormon doctrine, apostates and murderers are the only people who live an eternity in Outer Darkness. Apostates and murderers are guilty of the unforgiveable sins. Everyone else in history will spend eternity in one of the three levels of heaven about which Mormon doctrine teaches. My destiny would be an eternity in Outer Darkness alongside murderers. In the meantime, I would be ostracized from my community and, possibly, my family. Though the thought haunted me, something kept pulling me to seek answers.

A Sinful Nature...Say What?

One Sunday in January, our study led Gary and me to the root of most of our relational challenges: the question of human nature. We read through Romans 3:23: "All have sinned and fall short of the glory of God." I knew that I had sinned—that concept was not new to me. But Gary went on to say that the Bible teaches that we do not merely sin—our very nature is sinful. My lid came off when Gary looked me in the eyes and said, "Lis, the Bible teaches that our nature is sinful. I have a sinful nature. You have a sinful nature. The Bible teaches that all people are born with a sinful nature. Adam and Eve's offspring are all participants in their sinful nature."

A rebuttal leapt out of my throat with force. "I do not have a sinful nature!" I exclaimed. To say I was offended is an understatement. Something deep within me passionately fought this statement. I had a divine nature. As a begotten child of Heavenly Father and Heavenly Mother, I inherited their divine nature, giving me the capacity to exalt into godhood like them. Though I sinned at times, I was not sinful in nature. I had been taught that everyone on this earth had a divine nature and people are basically good.

Something about being called "sinful" unearthed a monster within me. I had internalized the Mormon second Article of Faith, which states, "We believe that men will be punished only for their own sins and not for Adam's transgression." As a Mormon, I was taught that Adam's sin did not infect his offspring because Christ's atonement erased it from humanity. I believed that everyone was forgiven through Christ's death on the cross; therefore, we were born into this life innocent, not sinful. This was what I had been taught about salvation. Jesus's death and resurrection covered the sin of everyone who would inhabit this earth. He freely restored our divine nature and gave us the ability to resurrect from the grave into an afterlife.

Gary pressed the issue further and read through Romans 5 with me: "Just as sin entered the world through one man, and death through sin, and in this way, death came to all people, because all sinned" (Romans 5:12 NIV). Gary continued reading, "For as through the one man's disobedience the many were *made sinners*, even so through the obedience of the One the many will be made righteous" (Romans 5:19 NASB, emphasis added). There it was again, that word I vehemently despised—*sinners*.

At the time, I didn't realize that my belief in my own divine nature had given me quite a lofty view of myself. The irony is that the life-style I was living at the time supported the truthfulness of this bib-lical argument. I possessed an uncanny capacity to disconnect those realities. Gary was painting a picture through the biblical story that showed that even if I was living obediently to the laws of God, I was born into this world with a sinful nature. I had looked for *life* in cre-ated things rather than in my Creator, who designed me to be filled with His love. He designed me to find my significance in Him, which would free me to love others and His creation rather than demand that His creation provide me with significance. The fallout of this act, which the Bible refers to as idolatry, is costly. We were designed for relationship with the Trinity and have our needs met in God. This would give us capacity to rule over creation and be completely other-centered, loving as the Trinity loves. Instead, we are caved in on ourselves because of sin. As a result, all of my righteous works were but filthy rags to God (Isaiah 64:6). I could not conceive of such a thing. As a Mormon, my works made me pleasing to Heavenly Father. Filthy rags? What are works for if not to make me acceptable to the Father?

Much to my chagrin, that night Gary kept attempting to show me the cost of sin. "The wages of sin is death, but the free gift of God is eternal life in Christ Jesus our Lord" (Romans 6:23). Gary said that when Adam and Eve ate from the tree of knowledge, seeking to become like God, they dethroned God from the center of their souls. This was the root of their sin. The cost of this was physical and spiri-tual death. I needed to break down this verse, as well as all the others

Gary had introduced me to, down into bite-sized portions I could digest.

Death

Death. I hadn't pondered death much because I had no fear of it. As a Mormon, I was confident I would be going to the highest of three heavens, which we called the Celestial Kingdom. My future Temple marriage would enable me to exalt to goddesshood[4] if I faithfully obeyed the laws and ordinances of the Church until my earthly death.

> What are works for if not to make me acceptable to the Father?

I hadn't pondered being spiritually dead either. Mormon doctrine taught me that, although everyone but murderers and apostates will end up in one of three levels of heaven, God the Father and His Son will only be present in the third level of heaven (called the third degree of glory). In this Celestial Kingdom, Mormons will enjoy *eternal life* if we have been faithful to the laws of the gospel and Temple ordinances. It is our obedience that makes us spiritually alive. A Temple marriage, faithful church attendance, keeping the Word of Wisdom, serving others, and paying a full tithe will secure eternal life—an eternity in the presence of the Father and Son. In addition to his claim that there will be three heavens in the afterlife, Joseph Smith claimed there will be three additional levels within the Celestial Kingdom. Only Mormons with a Temple marriage who have lived according to the laws and ordinances of the gospel will qualify for this level of exaltation. Occupants of the two lower levels of the Celestial Kingdom will be heavenly servants to those in the highest level. Everyone in the Celestial Kingdom will have eternal life.

In contrast to the Celestial Kingdom, God the Father will not be present in the lower two heavens. The first and second heavens, or degrees of glory, are called the Terrestrial and Telestial Kingdoms. Occupants of the Terrestrial Kingdom will be "honorable people who were blinded by the craftiness of men."[5] This group will include members of the Mormon Church who were "not valiant in the testimony of Jesus." It will also include those who rejected the opportunity to receive the gospel in mortality, but who later received it in the post-mortal spirit world. Occupants of the Telestial Kingdom "received not the gospel of Christ, neither the testimony of Jesus." These individuals will receive their glory after being redeemed from spirit prison. Occupants of the Terrestrial Kingdom will enjoy the presence of the Son, but not the Father. Neither the Father nor the Son will be present in the Telestial Kingdom.

Being married in the Mormon Temple was the doorway into being reunited with Heavenly Father, Jesus Christ, and my earthly family, to whom I was sealed in the Temple in the Celestial Kingdom. Eternal life had never been a free gift of God in my faith system. Eternal life was based on my faithful works. Salvation—overcoming death and resurrecting from the grave—was imparted by Christ's atonement and cost me nothing. But eternal life and becoming spiritually alive was up to me. And I believed I had the tools to make that happen. After all, my nature was divine.

The Mystery of Grace

I spent five months wrestling with this doctrine while scouring the Bible before I could begin to open myself to this biblical narrative. As if my doctrinal world was not being challenged enough, one of our next studies sent me into a tailspin. Gary took me to Ephesians 2:8-9 (NASB) to address how we reunite relationally with our Creator: "By grace you have been saved through faith; and that not of yourselves, it is the gift of God; not as a result of works, so that no one may boast." I was not acquainted with these verses. In fact, as Gary and I began breaking it down, I didn't know how to define *grace*. He defined grace as unmerited favor, something that cannot be earned.

"Lis, we aren't worthy of God's favor; it is a gift God extends to us freely." My wheels were spinning, attempting to comprehend what I was hearing. I had been taught a Mormon doctrinal verse that included the word *grace* and recited it frequently in church. It was the only context in which I remember hearing the word *grace* in church. "We labor diligently to write, to persuade our children, and also our brethren, to believe in Christ, and to be reconciled to God; for we know that *it is by grace that we are saved, after all we can do*" (2 Nephi 25:23, emphasis added). The Mormon third Article of Faith states that, "Through the Atonement of Christ, all mankind may be saved, by obedience to the laws and ordinances of the Gospel." What had lingered with me from Mormon doctrine was "after all you can do" and "saved by obedience to the laws and ordinances of the gospel." That is where our focus landed, and it informed our culture. I could make myself worthy with some effort. I was taught that I could bridge the gulf between Heavenly Father and myself.

I felt challenged to wade through these verses and teachings and break them down. Surely they would align in some way. I left this conversation with so many more questions than answers. What is salvation? What is eternal life? What has been given to us through grace? I vehemently opposed the idea of grace as a gift. I argued my stance confidently, thinking the idea that nothing is required of me to have eternal life was ridiculous. I thought it was preposterous and was mystified that anyone could believe that we didn't have to do something to make ourselves worthy for eternal life.

My World Unhinged

Terror simmered beneath the surface of every one of my conversations with Gary, occasionally causing my reactions to be volcanic in nature. After arguing with Gary about the nature of God and people for several months, I sought refuge in the belief that people may have different views of God, but despite our views we are all talking about the same God. Why should it matter if I assigned to God certain attributes and Gary assigned to God others? Weren't we all talking about the same God in the end? As we sat at Gary's dining room table, he challenged my thinking, "How can a God who is without a beginning or an end be the same God who had a beginning? How can a God who is spirit be the same God who is flesh and bones? How can a God who was once a man be the same God who has always been God, never changing?"

The questions made sense to him, but not to me. Somehow, I had the ability to suspend logic as we conversed about doctrine. Yet, at the time, I didn't know I wasn't being logical. Gary weathered my circular arguments with patience and grace. As I mulled over this particular issue over the next few months, an illustration came to me that helped me see the gap in my thinking:

> Lisa Halversen is eighteen years old, a tennis player at the University of Utah, from Salt Lake City, Utah.
> Lisa Halversen is 40 years old, a farmer's wife, lives in Missouri, and has three children.

These were two descriptions of someone with the same name. Was it possible for those people to be the *same* Lisa Halversen? As I looked at my argument pragmatically, it became obvious to me that the attributes we assign to God *do* matter. Just as it wasn't possible for those Lisas to be the same person, I saw that a god of flesh and bones who was a created being is not the same as the Trinitarian God who is uncreated and spirit. A god married to a Heavenly Mother, who begot every person on this earth in a preexisting world, is not the same God who is in an eternal community of love with His only begotten Son and the Holy Spirit, who proceeds from the love between the Father and Son.

Who was the true God?

My world seemed to come unhinged upon this realization. Who was the true God? My certainty about the Church of Jesus Christ of Latter-day Saints being the one true Church on this earth finally began to waiver. For five months Gary and I had battled, each of us fixed in our position. I had worked so hard to rationalize away the different views of God's nature that had been confronting me. I could not ignore the reality that the Mormon God and the God of the Bible are different. How would I know which one is the real Creator? Could I trust the Bible? Could I trust the Mormon doctrinal books? These questions lingered in the back of my mind. I had been taught that the Bible was fallible because Constantine and others had altered it. Therefore, it wasn't a completely reliable source of truth. A desire grew within me to research the reliability of the Bible as well as the Book of Mormon and other Mormon doctrinal books. A close examination would enable me to know which books and the teachings in them were true.

The Reliability of Scripture—It Matters

I researched archaeological and historical evidence to support the Bible and the Book of Mormon. I dug into the historicity of the books. I studied the life of Joseph Smith and wondered whether or not he satisfied the criteria to be an authentic prophet of God. As a Mormon, these were areas that weren't as important to me as my faith, which required believing in spite of my doubts. But as much as I hated it to be true, as I read the Bible and the Mormon Scriptures, I couldn't deny that they contained differing doctrines. Consequently, this process was necessary for me to establish a baseline for truth. I wanted to know which beliefs were true. I was in a "he-said-she-said" battle and needed to test the validity of the doctrinal sources to know in which God I would believe. Some of the significant findings for me were the following: discovering that there is no archeological evidence supporting the stories and locations in the Book of Mormon, while there is significant archaeological evidence to support biblical locations and events. I learned that there is more evidence of the Bible's authenticity than of any other book of antiquity. I was finding disturbing realities that caused me to doubt that the Book of Mormon was the Word of God, yet nothing could legitimately dismiss the Bible as a reliable historical book. A short list of some of the questions and facts that unsettled me as I thought about Mormon Scriptures is as follows:

- Where is the voice of Jesus in the Mormon Scriptures?

- Why does the Book of Mormon contradict the Bible on two of the major tenets of faith? 1. Who God is and 2. How one gets right with God.

- Why does the Book of Mormon say polygamy is an abomination when *Doctrine and Covenants* (both Mormon Scriptures) say polygamy is the new and everlasting covenant and eternal principle? These LDS scriptural sources contradict each other.

- Why does the Book of Mormon say dark skin is a curse (Alma 3:6-7)? The Bible repudiates all discrimination (Galatians 3:28).

- Why is there no DNA or other evidence supporting the idea that Native Americans are from Israel? The Book of Mormon teaches that Native Americans originated from Jewish settlers. However, current DNA evidence confirms that they are distinctly Mongoloid or Asian in origin.

- Why isn't there archaeological evidence for the Book of Mormon?[6]

- How can I trust the Book of Mormon to be the Word of God when there is no manuscript evidence to support it? On the other hand, there are 23,986 New Testament manuscripts alone, which provides significant support.[7]

- What is "Reformed Egyptian"? This language, which Joseph Smith claimed was the language of the golden plates from which he translated the Mormon Scriptures has never been discovered.

- No archaeological or genetic evidence has emerged to support the Book of Mormon's claims about the indigenous people in the book.

- The Book of Abraham, which Joseph Smith claimed was written by Abraham of the Bible and is canonized as Mormon Scripture, was determined by Mormon and non-Mormon Egyptologists to consist of Egyptian funerary texts.[8]

These were just a few of the issues I encountered on my journey. As I mulled over these realities with the Bible and Mormon Scriptures on opposite sides of a scale, I couldn't help but acknowledge that Mormon Scripture was weightless in its historicity and archaeological support. On the other hand, the Bible had significant archaeological evidence as well as historicity. I felt deceived by my Church and the way I had been indoctrinated to believe that the Book of Mormon was a reliable source text and superior to the Bible in reliability.

Another disheartening reality I needed to face as I studied to defend the authenticity of Joseph Smith as a true prophet of God was that I found him to be a man of very poor character. His practice of polygamy was disturbing to me.[9] I had always been taught that Mormons practiced polygamy because of an imbalance of males and females in the population. As I researched, I found that this was not the case.[10] As one fact stacked upon another, I was broadsided by waves of anger and fear. Why had all of this been hidden from me?

Throughout the spring and summer, I read and researched with fervor. Each discovery tipped the scale of truth toward the Bible, which only heightened my terror of my future. I knew I couldn't remain in a faith system that wasn't true, but the costs to leave would be enormous. Just the thought of sharing with my parents of my discoveries made me nauseous and frozen with fear. However, I could not shut down logic and thoughtfulness at this point. In any area of study outside of our personal faith, research, archaeology, and proof are considered valuable and necessary and good. I was bewildered as to why there had been such a willingness in my community of faith not to examine these problems and weigh the costs of facing them.

Perhaps the costs were too high, as was the weight that settled on my soul during this season of awakening.

God Incarnate

It had been five months since Gary and I had begun our once, carefree relationship. We had played hard, worked hard, and fought hard about doctrine. During these months, we stubbornly maintained our beliefs and argued our positions. I read Mormon doctrine, books by Mormons, writings of Mormon prophets, the Bible, and books by followers of the biblical Jesus. Occasionally, I mustered the courage to sneak into a Christian bookstore to acquire a new source of information. I was terrified that someone I knew might see me and my secretive questioning would be brought into the light. I was taught that external sources outside of our belief system were not valid in weighing the truthfulness of our beliefs. In addition, if these texts didn't support Mormonism, then Mormons considered them *anti-Mormon*. The Christian bookstore had a section of "anti-Mormon" literature, and I wasn't ready to be exposed.

But the more I read, the more clearly I could see the differences between the Jesus I had always known and the Jesus of the Bible. *Jesus was God*—that fact was inescapable. He said so Himself in John 10:30: "I and the Father are one." He proclaimed this to the Pharisees, who were about to stone Him for blasphemy—"Because you, a mere man, claim to be God" (John 10:33 NIV). There were numerous biblical references declaring there is one God and also that Jesus is God.

God had peeled back the next layer, light illuminating His Son, begotten of Him, His delight, fully man and fully God; not one in spirit as I had believed all my life, but one God. His majesty and mystery began to increase in my mind. How could I wrap my mind around something so contrary to my set of beliefs? Believing in the Mormon God wasn't ever mind-boggling, for He was so much like me, just ahead of me on the path of exaltation. I would be like Him one day. The picture of the biblical God that I encountered in my studies was beyond my imaginings. I needed more proof.

In his book *More Than a Carpenter*, Josh McDowell presents the case that we have three options when assessing the claim of Jesus to be God. He is either who He claims to be, He is a liar, or He is a lunatic.[11] As I read through the Bible and evaluated His character and life, His teaching and His purpose, it was evident to me that He was neither a liar nor a lunatic. He lived what He preached. He did not pursue His own glory, but the glory of His Father, so there was no personal gain for Him to claim to be God. He was all about His Father's glory. As I neared the end of the book, a sense of knowing began to form in my mind, my heart, and my soul. This Jesus was somehow God. The Father was somehow God. And the Holy Spirit was somehow God— the grandest mystery I had ever encountered.

A Portal into Another Reality

God, communicating himself, longs not to rest on the surface, but to feed and hold the whole person.[1]

IAIN MATTHEW, *The Impact of God*

*I*t seemed like layers of scales were being peeled off my eyes, one at a time, like peeling an onion. Bits of light shone where there had previously been only confusion, illuminating my mind and my heart to see what I hadn't seen before. The first layer that was peeled back enabled me to see that the Bible is God's Word. Through my research, I came to see it as the most reliable source of doctrine, which in turn released me to trust it. It felt like the deepest betrayal for me to no longer believe that "the Bible is the word of God, *as far as it is translated correctly.*" Instead, I believed it to be the Word of God, without disclaimer or caveat—infallible, God-breathed (2 Timothy 3:16-17). This began a revolution in my soul and my journey.

As the next layer was peeled back, I began to see myself more clearly. After five months of wrestling with the reality of my nature, I embraced the doctrine that I was not begotten of God the Father, but that I was affectionately crafted by Him for His delight and to reflect Him in this world. I could see that there was only One who has ever been begotten of the Father, and it is Jesus Christ. I embraced the idea that my nature is not divine, but sinful. This was actually a relief, because I could finally make sense of the shadow-side within me, which had felt so powerful throughout the past ten years. I had broken God's stunning and perfect law of love and made myself and others the center of the universe rather than Him. This idolatry had fractured my image-bearing design. I was designed to reflect God-colors and God-flavors on this earth, which would be me living fully as a human. I realized that though I was God's glorious creation, my nature was not basically good, but rather the natural inclinations of my heart were self-serving (Genesis 6:5), handicapping my ability to reflect God's power and love to this world.

Coming to this day of reckoning felt like I had climbed Mount Everest. But I came down from the mountain with a different vision of the world. Everything looked different after scaling rugged, unforeseen territory, using every ounce of grit within me to press on and not allow the dark clouds that often hovered over me to scare me into retreat.

Once I could acknowledge my sinful nature, I began to awaken to the gravity of the love of the biblical God. Throughout the spring and summer, I grew in awareness of the inclinations of my heart and my need for a Savior, not only to save me from death, but to lead me to eternal life. I spent the next season of my journey studying about the biblical Jesus. Gary so often shared with me that the God of the universe wants a personal relationship with *me* and desires for me to live in His kingdom, where love, grace, freedom, and life-giving power reign. I wanted to know who Jesus claimed to be. If Jesus wasn't my brother, then who was He? If His death didn't automatically replace my sinful nature with a divine nature, then what did it accomplish? What was this three-in-one God like, and would I want to know Him when I discovered Him? I was beginning to grasp that God loved me, really loved me, and created me to be in a loving relationship with Him and to reflect Him. I also understood that I was sinful, worshiping creation rather than the Creator. In doing so, I had handed myself over to forces that abuse that power. I had separated from this holy

God because I had centered my affections on everything but Him and wanted it to be that way.

My freshman year of college was coming to a close, and Gary was planning to head to California to play baseball for the summer. I wanted to understand the biblical God better, so he suggested that we meet with his pastor before he departed for the summer. So, before Gary left, we took a road trip to his hometown, Pocatello, Idaho, to visit his pastor who would hopefully help me understand the Trinity at least a little bit. I was slowly accepting that God was a boundless mystery, and yet He was still too mysterious for me to enter into relationship with Him and enter into His kingdom. Besides that, the terror of the thought of leaving Mormonism and how it would impact my relationships and family still encompassed me.

Gary and I arrived and sat across from his pastor in his church office. Gary had prepped him for my questions about the biblical God. I desperately desired to understand. The most vivid parts of our conversation were his pastor talking about water and eggs as metaphors for God.

"An egg is one egg, yet it has three parts—the shell, the white, and the yolk."

What?! my mind screamed. "God's like an egg?" I asked, completely baffled. "God just got more confusing to me if He is like an egg." I asked questions, hoping to wrap my mind around this concept. The pastor attempted to give me some answers. He moved on to his water metaphor.

"God is like water. Water has three different states in which it exists—ice, liquid, and steam. Even though it has three states, it's all water."

This metaphor for God also fell short and failed to help me make sense of the Trinity. Metaphors of states of water and an egg were not helpful. I now know that these metaphors left me even more confused because they're not accurate representations of one God who eternally exists in three persons at all times in a perfect community of love. I sat in the pastor's office beside Gary for some time, wrestling and questioning and wanting to catch even a glimpse of understanding. I left as bewildered and confused as I was when I had arrived. Yet, amid my frustration and confusion, I was being wooed by this God of love. This God, who created me to know Him, to relate to Him, to be free from the weight of the law under which I had lived all my life, was tenderly pursuing me. It wasn't long before Gary was off to California and I was alone in my search for the summer.

I began to understand my need for a Savior. I became aware of how, because of my sinful nature, I was content to center my life around created things, rather than around my Creator who designed me to be filled with His love. I needed a Savior who would completely cover me with His righteous work, not a Savior who would enable me to resurrect from the grave so that I could secure eternal life through my works. Coming to accept that there was nothing I could do to make myself spiritually alive and acceptable to a perfect and holy God was like taking a long journey into a foreign land. One step at a time, my puffed-up version of myself due to believing I had a divine nature was deflating, enabling me to see myself as well as God more clearly.

> Amid my frustration and confusion, I was being wooed by this God of love.

While walking this path, one of the most challenging landscapes for me to navigate was discovering that Jesus didn't make a distinction between salvation and eternal life. They were one and the same, used interchangeably. As a result, the verse from Ephesians, "By grace you have been saved through faith; and that not of yourselves, it is the gift of God; not as a result of works, so that no one may boast" (Ephesians 2:8-9 NASB), meant that eternal life (in the presence of the Father, Son, and Spirit) was a free gift. Only Jesus Christ, who was God in the flesh, could provide the perfect sacrifice necessary to enable me to fulfill the righteous requirement of God's law. The Mormon narrative captured in 2 Nephi, "For it is by grace we are saved, after all we can do," created a very different picture than the biblical narrative.

Over months of study, a picture formed in my mind of how these two narratives manifest at judgment day with God. As a Mormon desiring eternal life—eternity in the Celestial Kingdom—I would be clothed in my Temple marriage, paying a full tithe, actively attending church services, obeying the Word of Wisdom, faithful to Temple ordinances, serving others…the list would go on and on. Clothed in my acts of righteousness, I would be almost entirely covered in my righteous acts and fairly confident I had done enough to secure eternal life, but not one hundred percent sure. I would likely need Jesus to be my socks and shoes. His grace *makes up the difference* for my lack. I had heard it said over and over again in our faith community that Jesus makes up the difference.

> One step at a time, I seemed to decrease while the value of Jesus increased.

The picture that formed from the biblical narrative is that I would come to judgment before God completely covered in the blood of Jesus Christ. His righteousness would cover me completely. All the Father would see is Lisa, clothed in His Son's unblemished perfection. If I placed my trust in His work on the cross and received the gift of salvation and eternal life He extended to me, I would be made worthy through Christ's righteousness (1 John 5:11-15). The Father would pour His Spirit into me the moment I accepted His gift of eternal life through trusting in Christ's death for me. His Spirit would never leave me (Hebrews 13:5) but would indwell me every moment. I would be sealed for God and enjoy life in His kingdom. If I chose to walk into His kingdom through trusting in Christ's death, I would begin living an eternal kind-of-life with Him that would last throughout eternity.

Sometimes It Takes an Unexpected Encounter

I sat on my bed surrounded by books. Joseph Smith's *Discourses*, Bruce R. McConkie's *Mormon Doctrine*, and a few others lay beside me. But there was only one book that day that would take me to an intellectual and spiritual place I could not have imagined. As I had continued my search and wrestled alone through the summer, I was warming more and more to the invitation from the biblical God to enter into relationship with Him. He was still a complete mystery to me, but His story of redemption and the way of access into His kingdom had come to make sense. The only thing holding me back from accepting His invitation was my inability to comprehend Him more than I did.

The book was titled *Beyond Mormonism*. As I read its pages behind a locked door, I entered into the journey of James Spencer, a man who had converted to Mormonism in his twenties. He took me by the hand as he shared his story, giving me windows into critical parts of his journey toward God. He had been a faithful Mormon, marrying a lovely young Mormon woman in the Temple. He was blessed with children as well as Church responsibilities. He was a professor at a Mormon university called Ricks College (now BYU-Idaho) and the bishop of his local church congregation. He was progressing toward celestial glory, eternal life.

One day during a church service, he sat on the stand overlooking his congregation and the question, "Who is God?" popped into his mind. This question lingered relentlessly, catapulting him into a long, isolating journey of discovery. Like me, he needed to keep his questions quiet. His marriage and his job were both at stake. As I accompanied him through his search for truth, his story mirrored and framed each part of my own frightening journey. As I holed up in my room that hot August day, I felt the companionship of another who had come to the same conclusions I had as I sought truth. With each page of his story, I grew more aware of the holiness of God. His "otherness" became clearer and clearer to me. The gap between us expanded even more. I had come to believe that there was nothing I could do to make myself worthy to enter into the community of love of this Father, Son, and Spirit. God created me to invite me into this community. I understood that eternal life could not be acquired through any other means than my trusting in Jesus Christ's death as payment for my sin, becoming worthy through His righteousness. I believed that this loving God loved so deeply that He would not force His kingdom on me or anyone He had created. Though He offered the freedom to choose Him, I had come to see that He is always wooing, always extending the invitation to enter into His circle of love. I only needed to receive His invitation and walk into His kingdom. I had come to believe that I was created for friendship with Him as His daughter, and that once I accepted His invitation of eternal life through Christ, I would be adopted by blood into His kingdom at that point and throughout eternity. I believed my purpose was no longer to live a life of specific works that would enable me to exalt into goddesshood, but to be a God-reflector, reflecting His love, grace, and stewardship in the world. As I read the final chapter of the book, tears ran down my cheeks. This God was extending His invitation to enter into relationship with Him, to walk into His kingdom. I was filled with tension, because as close as I was to believing in Him, I was completely mystified by His nature.

"God, help me to understand You enough to trust You," I exhaled. Time passed. Then, gently, it was as if I was given a window into another reality—a vision of sorts. I saw Jesus on the throne; the presence of the Father and His Spirit encompassed what seemed like a sea of people before the throne. All were worshiping, bowed low before their King, proclaiming, "Holy, holy, holy is the Lord God Almighty; who was, who is, and is to come."[2] Over and over they repeated this phrase, offering all praise and glory to their God of love grace. I lingered in this space where everything I had wrestled with over the previous nine months came together in a grand crescendo. This Trinitarian God was not one that I could explain at the time; He was not one that I could comprehend. But as He invited me into this vision of Him, I witnessed the impact of a good and holy God on His people. I was overcome by the stunning reality that a God so perfectly "other" so longed for my friendship that He sent Jesus to bridge the gulf between us. I laid on my face and wept over my sin. I wept tears over how my skewed vision of Him had resulted in me worshiping myself and so many created things instead of Him.

"Holy, holy, holy is the Lord God Almighty; who was and is and is to come." It reverberated over and over. I was awestruck by God for the first time in my life. A Temple marriage could not get me into the kingdom of this God. Nothing I could do could make me worthy of His kingdom of perfect love. All of my study and research came together as I encountered this biblical God. He was the Creator. He was the good, good God who created me to share in His love. I realized that an incomprehensible God of love is meant to blow my finite mind. He is not anything like me, which makes Him worthy of my worship. He is unchanging, always has been God, and always will be God. And yet, He wanted me in His family and wanted to grow in friendship with me. As I lay facedown on my bed, weeping tears of sorrow and joy, my confession poured forth. "God, there is no other God but You. You are holy and I am not. I am full of sin which has separated me from You. I desire a relationship with You. I need You. Please forgive me my sins. Come into my life. Thank You that You are love. Thank You that You are faithful and will never leave me. In the name of Jesus Christ."

> I lay on my face and wept over my sin.

God had come close and graciously brought His kingdom near to me, so near that He was irresistible. I had toiled and fought and wrestled with Gary and God for nine grueling months, and now my soul was finally at rest. I took His hand and received His invitation to walk into His kingdom. For this one day, I was able to set aside the personal costs of my new relationship with Him and bask in His loving embrace.

I was fully and unconditionally loved. I was forgiven. I was accepted. I was covered in the perfect blood of Jesus. Because I was clothed in Christ's righteousness, I was worthy to be in His kingdom.

There was nothing I could do to make myself unworthy or to sever this relationship. I belonged to the Father. I had been given the gift of eternal life. Eternal life had begun for me and would never end. The arms of grace embraced me.

8

Love Is More Compelling

The Word became flesh and blood, and moved into
the neighborhood. We saw the glory with our own
eyes, the one-of-a-kind glory, like Father, like Son.
Generous inside and out, true from start to finish.

JOHN 1:14 MSG

*F*all semester of my sophomore year had arrived, and, on the outside, I resembled the girl who had walked onto campus a year
earlier. I still had my shoulder-length hair, athletic build, and golden
tan. But on the inside, something was shifting. I knew I wasn't the
same girl.

In August of my freshman year, I had walked onto campus as an
insecure young woman, seeking identity and meaning in relationships with guys and as a tennis player and a sorority girl. Now I was
a young woman who had a new identity, one beloved of God. I had
been a girl caught in a web of shame, seeking escape through altered
states of mind and relationships. Now I was a girl whose shame had
been absorbed by the biblical Jesus, and in its place, He clothed me in
His righteousness. I had been a girl hungry to be loved and accepted
unconditionally, seeking such love and acceptance in all the wrong
places. Now, in spite of myself, I was unconditionally loved and

accepted by God the Father through the blood of Jesus Christ. I had no power to alter my position with God. I could only hinder our fellowship. A year earlier, I had been a girl swinging between being worthy and unworthy—and then choosing to live unworthily. I was now a young woman made worthy of God's love and blessing through the blood of Christ. When God looked on me, He only saw Jesus and His righteousness. This was love and freedom. I was still wrapping my mind around this new identity (see 2 Corinthians 5:17). There was a monumental paradigm shift happening within me, which was stirring my desire to seek life in Him.

I found myself caught in tension between my old life, which was completely self-centered, and this new life, which was beckoning me toward a life marked by freedom to love God and others. I had turned to alcohol and guys for *life* and escape for so many years that it took some time before I was ready to surrender these idols.

Gary and I had been invited to a party thrown by some football players. We drank our usual drinks and danced to "Push It," Milli Vanilli, AC/DC, and hours of 1980s hits. We partied like we had always partied and had the senseless fun we always enjoyed. Yet, when I awoke the next morning, I felt something I had never encountered. I felt remorse and a discontentedness. I didn't feel shame, but rather, a deep conviction that there was another kind of life that would bring me the joy I was designed to inhabit. Still, I didn't know how to get there. Gary felt the same conviction. As I shared with him what was going on inside of me, he led me to a Bible verse that gave me some understanding of what was happening.

"Do not get drunk with wine, for that is debauchery, but be filled with the Spirit" (Ephesians 5:18). Was that why I was feeling so uneasy? As a Mormon, I had the Word of Wisdom to let me know it was wrong to consume alcohol. I had not looked into what the Bible had to say on the topic. From this verse, it looked like the point was to avoid getting drunk because something other than God's Spirit would be controlling me. When I saw that God desires His Spirit, who now lives in me, to fill me and be the primary influencer in my life rather than alcohol (or anything else for that matter), I understood the churning in my heart. This conviction within me was confirmation that God's Spirit had taken up residence in my body. Together, Gary and I decided to stop drinking and clean up our relationship. But then another weekend would arrive with another invitation to a party. Though I wanted to resist, something in me surrendered to the compulsion to seek life and freedom in the ways I had for three years. I felt captive to my old way of seeking life.

God was a persistent and kind pursuer. The morning after every episode of drunken partying, He was there as I sat in my unrest, extending grace and inviting me into another kind of life—a life fuller and more meaningful than I had ever known. Throughout the entire fall semester, I lived in this same rhythm, wondering if God would get impatient and be done with me. Yet, my wondering was always met with a gentle reminder, "I will never leave you. I am with you always" (see Hebrews 13:5 and Matthew 28:20). *How can He remain with me when I am living this way?* I struggled to believe and comprehend that this was my new God-reality. But as I read my Bible, His promises washed over my wrestling soul.

> The steadfast love of the LORD never ceases
>   his mercies never come to an end,
> they are new every morning;
>   great is your faithfulness (Lamentations 3:22-24 ESV).

It felt as though God was right next to me, speaking these truths into me. "There is therefore now no condemnation for those who are in Christ Jesus" (Romans 8:1). This was so challenging for me to grasp. I felt like I should be condemned. As I simmered in the reality that I was in Christ Jesus, I found myself desiring to draw near to Him. Because I was clothed in His righteousness, He covered my unrighteousness. Unlike the shame of my childhood church, where I needed to clean up before drawing near, this God was with me all of the time, whether I was in the light or the dark.

These convictions from God continued throughout my sophomore year as I sat in regret the morning after every party. And each night of abusing my chosen vices caused this biblical truth to seep deeper into my soul, uprooting bit by bit the gospel that I had believed the previous eighteen years. My life was altered by the realization that God was with me even when I looked for life outside of Him. There was nothing I could do to cause Him to remove His presence. It was a truth that I let envelop me as if I had plunged into a cool pool on a hot August day and sunk into the reality of being completely embraced by God. On some days, I was surprised He was still with me, living inside of me, just as He promised He would.

I Can't Believe I'm One of Them

Gary and I walked into the small wedding reception hall where Grace Community Bible Church held their Sunday services. I felt like a fish out of water attending church outside of a dedicated church building. Gary said I could wear whatever I wanted because God was more concerned with the condition of my heart than my wardrobe choices. I wore a skirt because wearing pants felt scandalous and inappropriate. The small congregation of fifty people embraced me warmly. We sang some upbeat songs and a hymn. Some people wore jeans and some women wore pants. I remembered sitting on the back row of that little Pentecostal church when I was fifteen years old on my Sunday School field trip. But, unlike then, I was no longer an outsider judging their appearance and music; I was one of them. The people at Grace Community embraced me as their own. Even so, everything felt awkward to me. Everything I had known about how to do church for eighteen years was different than this new church. I liked Grace and tasted God there. At the same time, each time I attended Grace, it was a reminder that I was walking away from my people and my culture. I had gained Christ and He was worth everything it would cost me.

> The people at Grace Community embraced me as their own.

The moments of spiritual grounding I experienced at Grace Community Bible Church caused me to be present to the reality that to follow the biblical Jesus might cost everything.

My sophomore year was marked by this pattern of living my old life, seeking pleasure and identity outside of God, and a growing desire to live another kind of life. I yearned to live a life with God, one in which addictions no longer had power over me. My back injuries were aggravated by the three hours a day of tennis workouts and strength training, so much so that I would awaken with my back frozen in pain in the mornings. The pain was worsening to the point that I began to contemplate the end of my tennis career. Tennis had been my life since the age of twelve. It had been one of the primary sources of my identity and community and to envision life without it was difficult. At the same time, I would awaken each morning with a stiff back, sometimes unable to move for thirty minutes. With my pain levels soaring, my mom was determined to use all of her resources to find me solutions that could keep me in the game. She brought me special dinners that she purchased from her neighbor who was a nutrition expert. They tasted earthy and were costly, so I ate. She bought me a magnetic mattress and comforter set in hopes of restoring my tissues. Despite all of the physical therapy and care, I was dealing with excruciating pain and it far outweighed the joy of playing the sport I had loved for so long. I felt my grip loosening on my racquet and prepared to surrender to my body's limitations.

Campus Crusade for Christ

As I approached the close of my sophomore year, Gary took me to a meeting on campus. He said there was a "campus ministry"—a new term for me—whose staff were there to help students grow in their relationships with God. I didn't know what I was getting myself into when we walked into that room in Bailiff Hall filled with about seventy-five students. Gary greeted people and worked the room with his natural wooing powers like a mayor. He introduced me as he went and then brought me over to some staff for an organization called

Campus Crusade for Christ (CCC). One by one, they greeted, me seemingly excited to meet me. As the meeting began, we sang songs about God that I would have labeled irreverent in my past. We were clapping and people were chanting with the songs.

Once again, I felt like a fish out of water. I hadn't experienced such playfulness in worship because Mormon worship is solemn. This God I was getting to know was so out-of-the-box. However, the students were warm. The staff were attentive to me. I felt welcomed and even embraced. I liked being with people who were living freely, but I was still in culture shock. One of the commonalities between Grace Community and CCC is the overwhelming feeling that I was letting go of my culture as well as my religion. Though people were warm and kind, I felt incredibly alone and like I was in a foreign land. Nothing felt natural because it was all so new. I didn't feel like I really fit anywhere.

After the meeting, a staff woman named Su Hecht asked if I would like to meet with her for a series of Bible studies about the realities God has promised me since entering into relationship with Him. I wanted to grow in my relationship with God and hoped she could help me figure out how to be free from my desire to party, because as much as I wanted to give it up, I felt powerless to overcome the urge to get drunk and make out with Gary. After living in the shadows for so many years, I couldn't seem to find my way into the light, even though Jesus, the light of the world, lived inside of me. Maybe Su could help me.

I met Su at the Student Union building for our first appointment. It had been eight months since I had invited Jesus into my life, and change was slow. I was holding my relationship with God close to me, and terror filled my body from head to toe at the thought of sharing my newfound faith with my parents and family. So I didn't allow myself to think about it much. I tucked the reality that I would one day need to have that dreaded conversation with my parents tightly into a compartment in the recesses of my mind and ignored it the majority of the time.

Su began leading me through our first Bible study. The concept that stuck with me was that because Jesus is faithful and had paid the penalty for my sin through His death, my relationship with God is secure. Sue gave me a word picture to help me visualize this security. Su placed one of each of our forearms side by side, then asked me to wrap my hand around her arm as she wrapped her hand around my arm.

"When you invited Christ into your heart, it's as if God gripped you this way. Though you can loosen your grip, God never loosens His. He's completely faithful to you and promises to never leave you or turn His back on you. When you walked into the kingdom of God, He promised to always be your God and king. He would never kick you out. You will never be unworthy of His love and acceptance and blessing because you are His beloved daughter through Jesus, who made you worthy."

I couldn't hear that reality about God enough. It was challenging for me to internalize that, even though I read it in the Bible. It was challenging to undo eighteen years of believing that personal worthiness was on my shoulders. I told Su about my drinking, and its power over me. She responded, "Sin does not affect your worthiness of His love because your worthiness is not based on you or your performance. You could never make yourself worthy. God's law of love is perfect and requires perfection. You could never satisfy His law despite how hard you work. Only Jesus was perfect, thus He was the only one who could satisfy God's perfect law. It required the Son, God incarnate, to satisfy God's law. Your filling yourself with alcohol is depriving you from enjoying Him as your source of life and all that comes with being filled to overflowing with His love. It affects your fellowship with Him, but not your relational security." Jesus was with me in the shadows. I had met Him in the shadows and there He remained with me as I drank myself into oblivion weekend after weekend. Slowly this reality was drawing me toward Him.

As summer approached, Gary and I decided to end our relationship. I knew that I was addicted to guys and I really wanted to allow

God to occupy the space I had given boys throughout my life. I was going to *walk with God*. I thought I was ready to surrender my vices to Him and give Him all of me.

And then, as quickly as I had made that decision, I began dating Mark, an offensive lineman on the football team whom I met in the weight room. He didn't have a religious upbringing and had no interest in God. I was gravitationally pulled toward him, and I suppose I wasn't desperate enough for God to fill these spaces in my soul that caused me to try, yet again, to secure my identity in one more relationship. I had always had a guy by my side. I didn't know who I was outside of relationship with a guy. The idea of being alone terrified me. Surely, Mark would satisfy my soul. Like my relationship with alcohol, addiction seemed to mark my relationships with guys.

9

Stunning Surrender

I do not understand the mystery of grace—only that it meets us where we are and does not leave us where it found us.[1]

ANNE LAMOTT

t the beginning of my junior year, my parents enabled me to rent a little house with a girlfriend and move out of my childhood home. This newfound freedom was amazing. My mom and dad knew that I was not attending the Mormon Church, and though it pained them, they had surrendered to the realization that they couldn't control me. We didn't talk about my spiritual state and I didn't want to. Because I hadn't experienced a lifestyle change since meeting Jesus, and wasn't surrendering my life fully to Him, I lacked the courage or motivation to offer them the news of my newfound faith. I mentally shelved the reality that one day, this conversation would need to occur. The thought brought a terror that I avoided most of the time.

Bewildering Pursuit

A CCC staff woman named Lisa Alexander began pursuing meeting with me at the beginning of my junior year. I was amazed that these people cared so much about my life with God that they would make it their profession to help me grow spiritually. Lisa was assigned to be my "discipler," which meant she was thoughtful about my spiritual growth and how she could encourage me toward greater intimacy with God. Lisa pursued me relentlessly, even as I failed to respond to her phone calls. She encouraged me toward God without any judgment as I continued to reside in the shadows.

Because Mark was not a Christian and had no interest in God, the time I spent with him caused me to see how much I desired a relationship with a man who loved God. I needed to compartmentalize God into a hidden space when I was with Mark because he had no interest in Him. This practice of compartmentalizing God into silence so that I could be with Mark brought an emptiness to our relationship. I didn't feel like I could live out of the fullest version of myself when with him or in my relationship with God. I already felt a growing discontentment with my way of living in my addictions, swinging from indulgence to brokenness before God.

As summer turned into fall and leaves turned colors and fell, despite my frustrating life pattern, I was being drawn to do life with Jesus. His gravitational pull was growing stronger than the pull of the places in which I had sought life outside of Him. His consistent kindness over the fourteen months since I had invited Him into my life, in spite of my darkness, was wooing me deeper into His heart. As leaves died and turned brown and crispy, I was waking up to how placing relationships, alcohol, and my athletic pursuits at the center of my world was sucking the life out of my soul.

You Want Me to Do What?

In mid-November, Lisa "caught" me and we met for a discipleship appointment on campus. We shot the breeze, talked about my life, and my relationship with God. And then Lisa dropped a bomb.

"Lisa, I think you need to consider telling your parents that you're a Christian."

My whole body froze. I felt like she'd just punched me in the gut. Words evaded me.

"You placed your trust in Christ over a year ago and it's understandable to take some time before sharing this kind of news with your parents. But if too much time passes, you begin to live a lie."

I've been living in lies as long as I can remember, I thought, my body still frozen. As Lisa continued to talk to me, her voice and the buzzing campus seemed to grow silent in the backdrop of my angst. This was my greatest terror. Why was Lisa telling me to do this? *I can't! I can't! I can't!*

When the sound returned to Lisa's voice, I heard her saying, "I'd like you to call our campus director, Dennis Brockman. He said he would be willing to walk beside you through this and give you some wisdom about how you might go about talking to your parents." She slid a small piece of paper across the table with his name and number scrawled on it. My gut felt hollowed out and my frozen body shook as I walked away from that appointment. I was too frozen to feel anything but the terror that had become my constant companion the year I questioned and researched Mormonism and Christianity. I had buried it beneath addictions for the past year. With one sentence, it had resurrected and overtaken my entire being.

Connection

Though I had a way of running away from people available and eager to help me grow in my relationship with God, my conversation with Lisa triggered something deep within me that I couldn't dismiss. I was haunted by the realization that I needed to tell my family about my newfound faith. I had smashed the thought into a little box, sealed the lid, and avoided it for over a year. Lisa had taken the lid off of the box, and as much as I wanted to hide it away again, I couldn't. I was restless as I drove from campus to my little home that day. I walked into the house, dropped my backpack in my room, and pulled the little piece of notebook paper out of my pocket. I had never met the man on the paper—Dennis Brockman. He was new to our Campus Crusade ministry that year and I had not attended a single meeting throughout the fall semester. But if he wanted to help me, I would take him up on his offer. I needed all the help I could get.

I dialed and Dennis answered. Dennis had moved to Provo, Utah, in high school and was one of the only non-Mormons in his high school. He attended the University of Utah nine years before I did and was intimate with Mormon culture and compassionate toward me. We talked for forty-five minutes about why it was important for me to consider administering the most brutal blow my parents would encounter in their parenting journey at that time.

I don't remember all the details of that call. What I remember vividly is that when I hung up the phone, my affections for Dennis Brockman were alive and well. I was drawn to his tenderness and wisdom and was completely crushed out on him. What in the world? I didn't have a category for what was going on in my body. My pattern with guys had always been 1) go out, 2) if attracted and having fun, make out, and 3) keep going out.

My affection for a guy had always included a physical attraction first. I sat on my little sofa while desire intermingled with fear. It all left me mystified and motivated to return to a CCC meeting and meet this man who had captivated my heart in forty-five short minutes through a phone line.

With a loaf of pumpkin bread and a pair of red Guess overalls in my arsenal, I walked into that room in Bailiff Hall for the CCC weekly meeting. Unlike eight months earlier, I was alone. Mark and I were still together, but I felt acutely the aching lack of spiritual connection between us and desired to be with a man who desired God in his life, even though I didn't feel like I was loving God very well. Lisa and Su greeted me, and then I walked to the front row where I found a seat. I sang and howled at a skit and anxiously awaited Dennis's appearance. Then a thirty-year-old balding guy stood in the front of the room to give a short talk. It was him. In spite of his balding head, my heart raced. I was captivated by him. In all of my twenty-one-year-old wisdom, I thought, *He's losing his hair and I still think he's beautiful...this must be from God.* I know—such deep thoughts. After the meeting, I introduced myself to Dennis and thanked him for his time and wisdom on our phone conversation that week. I conveyed my gratitude with my pumpkin bread and left that night with a greater desire for living another kind of life, a life in which I wasn't enslaved to relationships or alcohol or achievements. More than ever, I desired that Jesus would become my drug of choice. He was the only addiction I knew of that promised freedom rather than bondage. I didn't know how to get there, but knew I wanted to live in the freedom that Jesus offers me.

Throughout the last four weeks of my fall semester, Mark and I reached the end of our relationship. I tenderly shared with him that I wanted to be with someone who was also in a relationship with God. Mark said he understood and wouldn't ever be that kind of man. At the same time, I was working hard to stop drinking. Then December 20 came and with it, my twenty-first birthday.

At the Bottom

I was in my pajamas and had made it to 9:30 p.m. without a drink. I was feeling victorious. Then two girlfriends showed up at my door and declared that we were going out to celebrate. I resisted, yet without strong enough conviction to resist putting my arms through the sleeves of my shirt while they dressed me for our night of bar-hopping in downtown Salt Lake City. I felt powerless to overcome this lifestyle. We arrived at Port-of-Call, a bar I had fantasized about since my senior year of high school. We made it known that it was my birthday and drinks flowed freely as a result. I downed four shots and eight beers with my usual intent to get drunk.

Nothing. Not even a buzz. I had never had a problem transitioning to an altered state of mind. I had great capacity to hold my alcohol, I never grew sick, and I enjoyed mindless inebriation. As a result, this night felt like an out-of-body experience, yet I was fully in my body. Rather than enjoying my twenty-first birthday celebration, I was stuck being *present* and fully aware in the Port-of-Call bar. I was present to sloppy drunk guys who wanted to use me for their pleasure. I was present to take care of my drunk girlfriends. At the end of the night, I found myself in a dimly lit, urine-soaked bathroom holding one girlfriend's forehead while her body violently vomited out that night's source of "pleasure." This life in the shadows had felt life-giving in some way for so many years—but I now needed to be inebriated to endure it. On this night, in my sober state-of-mind, I wasn't enjoying the scene. I felt like I was chasing something untouchable and couldn't get there despite my valiant efforts. And to be sober in that space intensified the ache in my soul for something more than the life I had been living for so many years. The freedom that partying had brought me from the legalism of Mormonism had deepened my bondage, for it brought addictions with it. Instead of offering me power, I sacrificed my power to it.

When I arrived home at one in the morning, I walked into my bedroom and fell facedown on my forest green down comforter. I stretched out my arms with clenched fists and cried out to God, "I failed again. I don't want this addiction to rule me anymore. I am powerless to change. I need You to take away my thirst for alcohol. I want to be free. I need You take away my dependency on guys for my identity. Will You give me courage to be alone with You? I need You to clean my mind and make it new." I lay there weeping as I hit bottom with my Creator, knowing He was with me every minute since I had entered into relationship with Him. My Mormon god couldn't have remained with me amidst all of my *unworthy* behavior. But the biblical God was not a god who resided in Temples and places with the worthy, but a God who was my companion at every party, in every altered state, in every practice of immorality. He was always with me. I cried myself to sleep that night, under the covering of His love. I surrendered all of myself to my Creator, giving Him freedom to have His way in me. I don't think there's anything that could have delighted Him more at that moment. As I drifted off to sleep, I couldn't have imagined what was happening inside of me.

God had given me a heart transplant and washed my mind clean.

When I awoke the next morning, I was instantly aware that a profound shift had occurred in me while I slept. It's as if God had given me a heart transplant and washed my mind clean. He had smashed the chains that had been master over me. I knew my life-sucking addictions had lost their power over me, and in their place was a deep peace. This God was the only object I had centered my life around who didn't abuse the authority I had given Him over me, but invaded my entire being with His goodness and love. My desire to love and follow this Jesus was greater than all other desires. And that reality had never been mine before.

Road Trip

All I wanted was to be with other people who worshiped this God who never leaves His own and has the power to the break chains of addiction overnight. I had heard about a CCC Christmas Conference in Portland, Oregon. I managed to get registered, and on December 26, I was on a bus with a bunch of strangers for a fifteen-hour road trip. I had told my mom and dad that I was attending an interdenominational conference and there was even a van taking some BYU students to it. That was my attempt to soften the news that I was participating in a non-Mormon faith gathering. This was the beginning of my first step out of the shadows with them. I never would have had the courage to make this move before my twenty-first birthday. Since then, my desire to know and do life with God was growing greater than my fear of what I might lose as a result.

The news of my intention to attend the CCC conference was incredibly concerning to my mom and dad. They knew they couldn't stop me from going, but the waters beneath the surface were beginning to rumble in all three of us. We celebrated Christmas together, working to not bring attention to the elephant in the room. The following frigid, snowy day, I climbed onto a bus filled with strangers. Within hours, I felt surrounded by friends.

I dove into the experience with all of the fresh Jesus-vigor inside of me. I was in a sea of eight hundred students who set aside their

Christmas vacation to be at that CCC conference and, as far as I could tell, they shared my hunger to know Jesus more intimately. While in the first meeting, I discovered that CCC knows how to put on a conference and throw a party. The worship band brought down the house and the speakers' messages were compelling. There were so many memorable encounters for me throughout the five-day conference, but three stand out in particular.

Several days into the conference, someone tracked me down and said that my dad was on the house hotel phone waiting for me. Panic overtook my body. I felt pulled between the eight-year-old me who was still longing to please him and be delighted in by him, and the twenty-one-year-old me who was breaking his heart in order to walk the path I desired. It was the worst kind of torture. Someone led me into an open hallway where a large phone was mounted to the wall.

"Hi, Dad." My heart was racing.

For the next ten minutes, my dad asked me what was going on, who was speaking, by what authority they were speaking (since they weren't Mormons, my dad didn't believe they had the authority to teach me), and other questions that are a blur. He asked why I was doing this to him and my mom even though they had given me everything and the "fullness of the gospel." He believed I was being deceived by people and possibly joining a cult. I leaned against the wall, knowing nothing I could say would satisfy him, yet doing my best to be brave and honor him. As we said our goodbyes, I hung up the phone trembling and broke into tears. Nothing in life could prepare a Mormon girl for this moment, or the ones in the near future that were foreshadowed in that phone call.

The second most vivid memory from the conference was that Dennis Brockman was there. I think I had a DB monitor in my body that was on high alert. I wanted to be around him constantly. I began praying that God would bring us into a relationship someday. At the same time, when I broke up with Mark, I had committed the next year to God, boyfriend-free. It was a practice to which I sensed God was inviting me in order to find my identity in relationship to Jesus rather than a guy. I really needed and wanted to be faithful to that commitment, for I had never known myself outside of a guy. In the meantime, I could flirt and enjoy getting to know Dennis and, of course, pray for the miracle of marriage with this man.

The third most vivid memory from the conference was that Dr. Bill Bright, who is the co-founder of CCC, came to the conference to speak to us one night. He was a short man whose love for God seemed to ooze out of every pore. He stood on the stage and his love for Jesus poured forth from his entire being. He spoke about making and keeping Jesus as our first love. He shared moving stories about how CCC is sharing the love of Christ throughout the world. Then he invited us all to *come help change the world* by joining CCC staff. When he extended that invitation, something inside of me was stirred. Yes! I wanted to spend my life sharing this biblical God with everyone possible and helping them grow in that relationship. I want everyone to have the opportunity to know this God who is love, who stays with His people in the shadows of rebellion, failure, and addiction. I wanted everyone to know this God, who never leaves those who extend an invitation to Him to enter their hearts, who clothes the unworthy in the righteousness of His Son so they will always be worthy, and who is powerful enough to break chains of addiction overnight. I knew at that moment that my life trajectory was shifting significantly and I wanted to join the staff of CCC when I graduated from college. Before I did that, I was going to participate in a CCC summer mission project in San Diego, California, between my junior and senior years. I was excited. I was terrified. I was compelled by the love of God as never before.

I left that meeting knowing it was time to tell my parents about my newfound faith. And the thought of that brought nothing but dread. The upside of the situation is that I thought they would confront me because I had attended the conference. Like many families, my family can tend to avoid elephants in rooms. Even when they're gigantic, colorfully designed elephants trumpeting to be noticed. After returning back to Salt Lake City at the close of the conference, several weeks passed with neither of my parents confronting me. Was I really going to need to make an appointment and take the initiative? If we were going to face reality, it seemed I would need to be bolder than I thought possible.

10

Tumultuous Waters

We are wired to grow, and all growth stretches us
beyond our comfort level. Comfort is the absence of
tension; growth requires a swim in murky, dangerous
waters.... There are no safe risks. There is no growth
that comes with a guarantee of success.[1]

DAN ALLENDER

On January 12, 1991, my parents and I walked into the small Kyoto restaurant for a lunch date. I had strategically chosen this spot as the place I would share with my mom and dad the news that I had kept locked away for sixteen months. When I mustered the courage to invite them to lunch a few days earlier, I knew that I needed to be in a public place that could contain the emotional storm that I foresaw would greet me this day. As I had thought about this day for the past several months, compassion for my parents seemed to hold hands with the anxiety inside of me. They had been faithful to their religion. They are zealous Mormons who eat, sleep, drink, and breathe their doctrine. They had brought me up in their faith system with diligence. They love their church. This compassion and anxiety would intermingle for the following year-and-a-half.

I had just given my dad a tennis lesson, which felt like an hour of normal and calm before the storm. I loved teaching him and playing with him. As I fed him each ball, I knew I was one ball closer to walking into mysterious, unchartered territory. Though I felt fearful, there was also a peace in knowing that my God was going to be there with me—within me and completely surrounding me, promising to never leave me or forsake me (Hebrews 13:5). This intimacy I was experiencing with God was the greatest high I had ever known. I wanted more of Him, and He was beckoning me to follow Him into mystery.

Our hostess took us to a booth in the small restaurant. I ordered my usual chicken donburi and sought to be present in small talk with my mom and dad until our lunch was served. I wondered what was swimming through my parents' minds. I wanted it to take forever for our server to bring our food, and I also wanted it to be now so we could bring closure to this conversation. Butterflies filled my abdomen, fluttering manically. Then our food was placed before us and I wanted to run away and cry. At the same time, the love of God compelled me into the conversation. I wanted to honor my parents and no longer hide from them. I gave us time to eat some of our meals because I knew that after I shared my news, we all would lose our appetites.

After consuming a good amount of my donburi, I verbally stumbled as I turned the conversation, telling them that there was something difficult and significant I wanted to share with them. After some more fumbling, I said, "There's something I need to share with you. During my freshman year, Gary asked me how I knew Mormonism was true." I continued to share about my doctrinal search throughout the previous two years. As I brought that story to a close, I said, "Mom and Dad, I have placed my trust in Jesus Christ alone for my eternal life."

My mom gasped and exclaimed, "You've left us! You've left the family!" and then tears streamed down her face as she wept out her grief. Not even the Kyoto restaurant could deter the expression of loss that a Mormon mom feels at the revelation that her daughter is choosing another path of faith than the one she has embraced throughout her entire life. My heart beat so vigorously I thought it might beat right out of my chest. I was so surprised by my mom's words that I couldn't find any words to offer at that moment. I couldn't have anticipated what my mom's first words to me would be in response to my offering, but "you've left the family" had never crossed my mind. I didn't want to leave the family. In fact, my heart had never been more turned toward my family than now. Jesus was growing in me a desire to love them rather than protect myself. And loving them required honest disclosure and an invitation to journey with me into the mysterious territory ahead. Leaving Mormonism was messy and pain-filled for everyone touched by my decision.

I was emotionally rattled and my body shivered from emotion. As my mom wept, my dad began to talk doctrine with me, which we were both too emotional to do well. We were on opposite sides of a doctrinal line in the earth that felt like a chasm so wide nothing could bridge the gulf at that moment. Our emotions were raw, each of us doing our best to edit them because we were sitting in a booth at the Kyoto restaurant. I don't know how long we stayed there. I don't remember leaving. My emotional memory holds me in that booth in the Kyoto restaurant to this day.

> I wanted more of Him, and He was beckoning me to follow Him into mystery.

Apostasy

I was officially an apostate of the Mormon Church. The eternal cost of apostasy for an ex-Mormon is spending eternity in Outer Darkness, or what I viewed as hell, with murderers and other apostates. This cost was one of the doctrines that kept me searching and wrestling with my beliefs for so long before embracing biblical Christian theology.

One of the devastating results of my apostasy is that I had broken our family's eternal destiny of being together forever in the Celestial

Kingdom. I think this is what was beneath my mom's initial response to me, "You've left us! You've left the family!" My parents believe that our family was sealed throughout eternity because of ordinances my parents performed in the Temple. However, it was dependent upon all of their children remaining faithful to the Church's doctrines and lifestyle. I was the first to be unfaithful, and nothing could have prepared my parents for that blow.

Mormons believe sincerely that their church is the only true Church on the face of the earth. Thus, it doesn't occur to devout Mormons that perhaps someone might apostatize based on an *understanding* of doctrine, or that there is actually a thoughtful process that led me to conclude that Mormonism isn't true based on my understanding. From their perspective, if I understood, I would believe. From my parent's perspective, I fell prey to Gary's false teachings and was victimized and deceived into apostasy. My parents' hope was to help dissolve my assumed doctrinal misunderstandings and restore their eternal family. My hope was that we would weather this storm with our relationship intact. When my parents undergo their interview with a church authority to have their Temple recommend renewed every three years, one of the questions they are asked is, "Do you associate with apostates?" Now their daughter was one of those. It felt like I was no longer the only one whose firm foundation had turned to quicksand.

Emotional Desolation and a Cross

The following day, my parents asked me to study the Bible with them following our weekly Sunday family dinner. It was a mess. *We* were a mess. As expected, we did not see eye to eye about doctrine. My mom was in one of the rawest emotional states I had ever seen. My parents told me that they believed I was in a cult and going to Outer Darkness. They also expressed that I was tearing our family apart.

"Where did you attend church today?" my mom asked.

"The Evangelical Free Church," I responded.

"What did they teach? What did you learn? Why can't you come to church with us? Did you feel the Spirit when you were there?" my mom quizzed in rapid fire.

"Who taught you?" asked my dad.

"The pastor gave a sermon," I replied.

"By what authority is he teaching you Scripture?"

"Under the authority of Jesus Christ," I responded.

Their questions persisted and then my dad quoted a bunch of Bible verses while anxiety filled every cell of my body. I wanted to stay in this with them because our relationship was so important to me. At the same time, everything in me felt the urge to run out the front door and escape the onslaught of emotions and questions. Anxiety engulfed my body throughout my stay.

Throughout the next six months, encounters like this one happened frequently. Each time I joined my family for dinner, I lived in the tension of knowing that arguments might break loose at any moment. Each one of these encounters was as jarring as the previous one. I never grew used to them. Perhaps because of the intensity of communication between my parents and me during this season, my siblings didn't engage in the conversation, which was a relief.

Sometime following my conversation with my parents at the Kyoto restaurant, I received a thick envelope in the mail. My heart raced as I studied the return address. It was a six-page letter from my mom. I wanted to keep the contents of the letter stored safely inside that envelope where they couldn't touch my heart. The thought of letting those pages out of captivity terrified me. Hands shaking, I pressed into my fear and tore open the envelope. As I read, I experienced my mom's angst, devastation, and ache filling each page. In her desolation, she expressed that I had "ruined the family, killed all of the joy between us as well as in her life, and used her for her unconditional love." As I continued to read, I was given an ultimatum and "would be expected to attend church with them weekly or else." The weight of her words crushed me. *I've destroyed the family*—how did I have that much power? *Used them for their love.* How had I done this? *Or else.* Or else *what?* These were words I feared would come. I had heard stories of Mormons cutting off relationship with apostate family members and I couldn't imagine how I would survive that. In addition, my parents still supported me and were paying for my college education, which meant I was still very dependent on them.

I sat on my love seat and tears trickled down my face. And then something deep within me broke and tears turned to weeping. I think I wept over the many painful encounters I had had with my parents since I'd shared my newfound faith with them. There was something in me that wouldn't allow myself to feel the full impact of the brokenness of our interactions because I needed to keep going, needed to keep the armor in place to be able to handle the next stressful interaction. But this letter from my mom was the blow that pierced the deepest parts of me and tears that had been dammed now spilled forth. As I wept on that couch, I sensed that Jesus was with me. The one thing I knew is that in this emotionally icy winter, my God was always with me.

As I pondered my response to my mom's letter that night, I decided I would write back rather than talk with her face-to-face. In our face-to-face conversations, emotions that prevented us from listening and seeking to understand each other escalated swiftly. I also think my parents were in a state of loss so deep that it was challenging to relate in any other way. A desperation to win their daughter back to their religion laced each of our encounters.

The day after I had received my mom's letter, I had planned to spend the day at home. This meant that I could wear my new gold cross around my neck for I didn't have plans to see family. A deeply significant day for me, since deciding to follow the biblical Jesus, was the day I went to the Christian bookstore to pick out a cross necklace. As I was growing up in Mormonism, I learned the message that the cross was an almost evil symbol and Mormons don't wear crosses. We didn't have crosses on top of our churches like Protestant churches, nor did we have them inside our churches. Tall, skinny steeples adorned the rooftops of our church buildings with the Angel Moroni atop the Temples. My Sunday School teachers would say to the class, "If my child was killed in an auto accident, would I wear a crashed-up car around my neck?" in defense of our anti-cross position. It had been instilled in me that it is wrong to display a cross anywhere and that to do so was sacrilegious.

As I researched biblical Christianity, I realized that it was on the cross where Jesus was made to be sin so that in Him, I could become the righteousness of God (2 Corinthians 5:21). It was His work on the cross that enables me to become His righteousness; therefore, I would always be worthy of His love and acceptance in spite of myself. As I owned the fact that my nature was sinful and not divine, I grew aware of the pricelessness of the cross of Christ. It became a treasure to me rather than something to be abhorred. As I studied the Bible, one verse about the cross tucked itself into my heart, "May I never boast except in the cross of our Lord Jesus Christ, through which the world has been crucified to me, and I to the world" (Galatians 6:14 NIV). Not only was it precious to me, but the cross was the one thing in which I was exhorted to boast. This was one of those radical cultural paradigm shifts for me as I made my pilgrimage out of Zion. The cross wasn't sacrilegious, but the representation of how I am to live as a Christ-follower, how I am strengthened, and how I am empowered.

As I scanned the numerous crosses on display at the bookstore, I chose one that possessed presence. It had a Gothic flare and because it was 1991, yellow gold was all the rage. I loved the feeling of it against my skin and the constant reminder of Jesus and that I belonged to Him. Despite its preciousness to me, it took time before I would muster the courage to wear a cross in the presence of my family. In fact, it was about twelve years before I entered a family gathering wearing a cross. All of these instances of living more authentically before my family, like wearing a cross necklace, required wading through a lifetime of beliefs and possible relational strain before I could take the plunge.

As I dressed for the day, I wrapped my cross necklace around my neck. An hour later, the doorbell rang. When I opened it, my mom was standing on the porch, looking like she'd been crying nonstop for days.

"Mom!" I exclaimed.

She gasped. "What is that *thing* around your neck?" she cried. Then, in dramatic display, she gasped again and lunged toward me with an outstretched arm aimed right at my neck. I impulsively stepped backward to protect my cross. She crumpled on the threshold of my doorstep and wept as I stood over her with my heart racing in my chest. My mom wept there in a heap of anguish as if the little cross just above my heart had pierced hers. When she mustered the energy to rise, I invited her inside to talk. As with each of these encounters with my parents, part of me wanted to talk so we could salvage our relationship, and the other part of me wanted to run and escape. It all felt like *too much.*

Words cannot capture the rawness of emotion between us. Despite the feelings my mom expressed in the letter, she ached to stay connected, which is why she showed up on my doorstep that day. She said that she'd been in turmoil because she hadn't heard a response from me. One of the profound challenges for us when we're neck-deep in our stories of loss is that we aren't able to see out of our story and into another. We talked and shared tears and came together with an embrace. I felt compassionate toward her, yet also pierced by her words. My mom was dying to her dreams for me and fighting with all of her might to win me back to the Mormon Church. As she walked to her car after our tense visit, it occurred to me that it would probably be preferable for my parents if I were an addict rather than a Christian. For if I was an addict, they could place me into a rehab center and still feel some illusion of control—and I would still be a Mormon.

Feasting and Friends

One practice that became a bedrock for me that spring was to read the book of Galatians each morning before I began my day. It was like my spiritual Krispy Kreme. It was my lifeblood fueling my ability to persevere. That might sound cheesy, but it was one of my survival practices that enabled me to endure the relational brokenness and strain that resulted from my decision to follow the biblical

God. Reading Galatians was like steeping my mind in the freedom Jesus offers me and the richness of His grace that covers me. I also plunged into the CCC community, which became like a family to me. Their consistent love and embrace restored my broken heart day after day.

Created to Endure

Several months after our conversation at the Kyoto restaurant, I walked into the University of Utah LDS Institute of Religion building to meet with my dad, the director of the Institute, my pastor, and Bob, a former Mormon from Salt Lake City. I had been introduced to Bob sometime during my doctrinal search and was grateful for the insight he provided. There I sat, surrounded by four men to discuss doctrinal issues. I thought Bob might be able to help my dad understand where I was coming from, and my dad thought it would be helpful to partner with the director of the Institute. Everyone made their introductions and then the director suggested we pray together. "It would be good to open with prayer," Bob said, "but we want to be the ones to pray because you pray to Satan."

BAM!

I was screaming on the inside. Why did he think he needed to say that?

Everything in me wished I could disappear and erase Bob's words from the space they occupied. I felt horrible that he made that comment, but I was powerless to turn back time and erase the unloving accusation. I sat through that meeting, next to my dad and surrounded by three other men wishing I could say or do something that would bring peace and understanding. We were all passionate about our beliefs, and the doctrinal gulf between us was so wide nothing could bridge it. Tension filled the room throughout the meeting and it only served to show that we were at an impasse with our beliefs. In what felt like a winter storm, peace eluded us as we fought for our beliefs. The grace in this intense season of me transitioning out of the Church is that we kept fighting for each other as well.

As winter faded into spring, depression settled upon my mom. One day my phone rang and my dad was on the other end of the line, "Lisa, Mom and I are seeing a counselor. His name is Dr. Scott. He said that he could more successfully help us if he could have one session with you. Would you be willing to see him?"

"Of course I would," I replied.

I walked into Dr. Scott's office the following week. He was in his sixties, tall and gentle. We shook hands and he thanked me for meeting with him. After some introductory conversation, Dr. Scott asked me if I would share my story with him so that he would have a fuller picture of our journey.

For the next thirty minutes, I invited Dr. Scott into my life. Being a fairly new Christian, I must have said the name "Jesus" in every other sentence. I shared about my longing to be worthy, my life in the shadows, and meeting Gary. I shared about my questioning, my searching, and my choice to place my trust in the biblical Jesus alone for eternal life. I shared about my twenty-first birthday, the night I surrendered my addictions to God and the freedom His revolutionary love had brought to my soul. I talked about Campus Crusade for Christ and lunch with my parents at the Kyoto restaurant. Then I shared stories of interactions between my parents and me the previous five months—the heartache I caused them by choosing a different faith from theirs and the emotional and relational fallout.

As this story came to a close, we sat in silence for a moment.

Then Dr. Scott broke the silence, "Lisa, children weren't created to endure the situations you've encountered with your parents these past months. You're under an enormous amount of stress. I'm wondering how you've endured."

I don't remember my response. Dr. Scott's gaze and compassion helped me release a breath I didn't know I was holding.

He said with sincerity, "Lisa, it's going to take a miracle to shift your parents' thinking, but I believe in miracles." Tears filled my eyes and then I sobbed. There was something so tender about feeling seen and embraced by this man who was a stranger to me only an hour earlier. He continued, "Before you leave, let's talk through forgiving your parents."

"Forgiving my parents?" I asked, "I've already done that. I forgive them each time they hurt me."

I don't think he believed me because for the next five minutes, Dr. Scott asked me questions to find something I might be holding against my parents.

"Well," he said, a bit bewildered, "it seems you have forgiven them. Hearing from you will help me as I work with your parents. Thank you for coming."

> There was something so tender about feeling seen and embraced.

Almost two and a half years later, our family was driving to Lake Powell in Southern Utah for a week-long vacation before I moved to Orlando, Florida. My mom had asked if she and I could ride together alone for part of the trip. Although tense conversations were much less frequent than they had been, I still felt nervous about traveling alone with my mom for hours. She'd driven me all over from California throughout the Intermountain Region for tennis tournaments during my teenage years. Though there was greater peace between us then, at that time I was living in the shadows and hiding much of myself. Now, I was no longer hiding and was more turned toward my family than I had ever been. Ironically, this also meant there was more conflict and unrest than there had been.

About an hour into the ride, my mom surprised me. She said there was something she'd been wanting to share with me for a long time.

Then she said, "When I returned to see Dr. Scott after your visit with him, he said some pretty remarkable things to me that I want to share with you. He told me that in his many years of counseling, he's rarely met someone so committed to Jesus Christ and so committed to her family."

"Wow." I replied. I was stunned to hear that. *He probably isn't counseling many young Christians whose lives have been rocked by the extravagant love of God as mine had been,* I thought.

"He shared with me a word picture. He said it's as if you are walking on a tightrope and Dad and I are beneath you trying to pull you down. If we continue to do that, we may injure you permanently one day. He encouraged us to let go and allow you to walk the path you need to walk."

I was stunned. I thought it was significant for a Mormon therapist to give Mormon parents that counsel. I wasn't expecting my mom to say that.

"He helped me to see what I couldn't see and that was a turning point for me," she said. "It was like death to know that I had lost control and was powerless to change your mind. And it's still hard for me. But Dr. Scott was right."

Though my decision to follow the biblical God ushered my mom into deep darkness and loss, she has wrestled fiercely with her pain and questions in hopes of better understanding, accepting, and loving me.

Pandora's Box Has Been Opened

Throughout the spring of my junior year at the University of Utah, Mormon friends I had grown up with began to hear that I had converted to Christianity. In Salt Lake City in 1991, it wasn't common for Mormons to apostatize. It was even more uncommon for a Mormon to convert to Christianity. I was falling deeper in love with Jesus with each new day and following Him was worth all of the relational costs. However, the moments of confrontation with others over my choice to leave the Mormon Church were emotionally jarring every time. It costs a great deal to leave the Mormon Church, so much that it often takes years to muster the courage to make the leap. I don't know any post-Mormon who has made that choice flippantly. Yet, the active Mormons I know are unable to see what it costs.

I ran into Blake on campus one day that spring of 1991. We had been in the same ward since I moved to Utah from California in 1978. Blake had been one of my close friends during various seasons of our lives. Throughout grade school, we faced off during recess on the football field, equally fierce and determined. (At our twentieth high school reunion, while having lunch with Blake and his kids, he reminisced about how I was the one person who beat him in the 100-yard dash and the President's Physical Fitness challenges. We laughed as he said he always wanted to beat me.) We enjoyed growing up together. Our paths didn't keep us closely tied through high school but we always attended church and youth functions together. I hadn't seen Blake for probably a year and was happy to bump into him.

We greeted each other and caught up a little bit. Then he shared he'd heard a rumor that I had left the Mormon Church. I told him that I had converted to Christianity. He lifted his hands above his head and began waving them wildly around then asked, "So, do you raise your hands like this when you sing now?"

I laughed it off, pretending I wasn't affected. My heart felt the blow of his expression and I was caught off guard.

Then Blake asked with a hint of sarcasm, "So do you have one of those little fish on your car now?"

"Yes, I have one of those fish," I replied feeling awkward.

Our conversation didn't last much longer. He could have asked me ten other questions like, "What caused you to leave the Mormon Church? Why would you convert to Christianity? What has that been like for you?" Instead, I walked away feeling punched in the gut. I understood where he was coming from. Because we weren't exposed to other churches growing up, other than our wild and crazy field trip to the Pentecostal church, the extent of our experience of Christianity was seeing the televangelists on TV. I thought *they* were the crazy ones raising money and shouting "hallelujah!" while people fell backward to the ground after being bonked on the head by their pastor. To a Mormon girl, the TV evangelists were bizarre and off-the-wall, and I associated all Christian clergy in their category because of my lack of experience. Joseph Smith claimed that when he sought out God's wisdom as to what Protestant denomination he should join, which led to his first vision,[2] he claims Heavenly Father said of them and their leaders in his first vision, "All their creeds are an abomination in my sight; that those professors are all corrupt" and that "they draw near to me with their lips, but their hearts are far from me, they teach for doctrines the commandments of men, having a form of godliness, but they deny the power thereof."[3] Even though I now had the mind of Christ (1 Corinthians 2:16), I still found myself facing-off with the beliefs I know Mormons hold about apostates, making for a continuous battle with shame. I knew what they thought about those who leave and the judgment that is difficult to avoid. *They didn't seek with a sincere heart. They looked for answers in non-Mormon sources. They didn't want to pay tithing anymore. They want to drink alcohol, coffee, and tea. They don't like getting up for church on Sundays. They've been deceived by false doctrines.* I've experienced these simpleminded comments about apostates throughout my entire life and rarely, if ever, do I hear a response from an active Mormon that demonstrates genuine curiosity, like:

"I wonder why they left?"

"I wonder what would cause someone, for whom it cost everything, to leave the Church?"

"What would cause someone to risk losing their family and friends, while leaving behind their culture, community, and beliefs, to have the courage to depart from the Mormon Church?"

Living a sheltered religious life as the majority religious population creates a kind of "groupthink" that doesn't foster curiosity, but rather perpetuates judgment. It is as if the moment the knowledge that "a member" has left the Church is discovered, an auto-play button is pressed in the brain with a handful of reasons for this apostate's lack of holiness. In their confident "knowing," they excuse themselves from curiosity. This is one of the realities I have navigated throughout the past twenty-seven years since I left the Church. In my less victorious moments, shame has climbed me like a tree.

Another memorable encounter with my Mormon friends happened on a Sunday during that same spring. Kate's younger brother's mission farewell was happening in church that day and she invited me to come to the open house at their home afterward. Mission farewells are one of the most significant days in a young Mormon man's life. It's almost equally significant for the entire family. As they enter into the missionary rite of passage, the missionary is the main speaker in church on the day of his farewell. He has been ordained an elder and is no longer known by his first name but will be *Elder Last Name* for the following two years as he serves his mission. Following the church service, friends and family gather at the missionary's home for a luncheon and celebration before the elder departs for the Missionary Training Center (MTC) in Provo, Utah.

I pulled my little red Nissan Sentra into the long row of cars in front of Kate's family's home. Though some distance had grown between Kate and me as we entered into college life, we saw each other occasionally and I still treasured the soul sister she was to me for six years of my life. She was a faithful and fun friend. As I climbed out of my car, I thought about the fish on the rear of it and how it took courage to leave it on display while I was in this place. I had been attempting to connect with Kate for some time, but had only been able to leave messages with her dad. I walked into the home that had been my second home throughout junior high and high school. This was the first time I would be interfacing with all of these high school friends since I had become a Christian, so I was feeling like a fish out of water. Most of the guys present had recently returned from serving their two-year missions for the Mormon Church and Kate would soon serve one as well.

When Kate and I hugged, I said, "Girl, I can't believe you haven't returned my calls. I've been attempting to connect with you."

"You have? I didn't know that you called," she replied matter-of-factly.

"I left messages with your dad," I said.

"Well, he never gave them to me."

I felt a little insecure in our friendship since leaving the church and was relieved to know that she wasn't purposely avoiding me.

We ate and socialized and caught up on life. Later in the afternoon, I wandered into the kitchen to greet and hug Kate's mom and dad, who'd been my second parents for years. When I hugged her dad, I hazed him for not giving Kate the messages that I had called to connect with her.

Surprised, he replied, "I gave your messages to Kate."

His six words took the wind out of me. *Why would she lie to me about that?* She *had* been avoiding me on purpose. Rejection and shame pierced my heart, and it was all I could do to muster the composure to leave the party gracefully. I didn't have the courage to follow up with Kate and have a conversation about her avoiding me. Neither of us could find words or the courage to have these difficult conversations. There were about ten more painful interactions with different people during that afternoon, them making fun of my faith in some way or another. Kate was growing her roots deeper into Mormon soil while I had completely uprooted mine and planted myself in another world with a language, beliefs, and culture foreign to the one we had all known and been comfortable with all our lives. I didn't yet feel at home in my mainstream Christian culture, but I was thankful that I felt loved and embraced by my CCC community.

> Living a sheltered religious life as the majority religious population creates a kind of "groupthink" that doesn't foster curiosity, but rather perpetuates judgment.

A DT-What?

On April 23, 1991, near the close of my junior year, Dennis approached me in the student union building. After talking briefly, he said, "After the meeting tonight, I want us to get in your car, go get frozen yogurt, and have a DTR." I didn't know what DTR meant, but something in me knew it would be a significant conversation because my stomach dropped to the floor and I almost choked on the pretzel I was eating. As we ate yogurt at the Sugarhouse Golden Spoon that night, Dennis defined DTR: "define the relationship."

My dream was coming true. Maybe I filled Dennis's thoughts in some small version of the way he filled the pages of my journal.

"Lisa, I really enjoy our friendship, and feel encouraged by you. I have a wonderful time with you and enjoy the time we spend together. I'm also attracted to you. God hasn't given me the green light for a commitment, but I would like to continue to spend time with you."

Without a pause I exclaimed, "Killer!"

We remained friends over the next nine months with the freedom to spend time with whomever we desired. However, Thursday nights were often dedicated to country swing dancing with a group of friends. When we came to the point where I really didn't think Dennis was ever going to see a green light to pursue me with any sort of passion, he surprised me with another DTR. As he swung me across the dance floor, he pulled me toward him and said, "Let's dance one more dance and have a DTR."

I was annoyed at this point. He had been so reserved in pursuing me, which I completely understood given that he was directing the CCC ministry on campus and directors weren't supposed to date students. Also, he was nine years my senior, so there was a bit of maturity gap. Oh, and then the factor that I was just venturing into my relationship with Jesus in a way that influenced all parts of me and my life. Even so, I was annoyed that it took him so long to decide if he wanted to pursue me or not because those nine months had felt like years to me.

"You wing these DTR's on me at the oddest times!" I exclaimed. "We aren't waiting. You can tell me now what you want to say."

After telling me how attracted to me he was and the many wonderful things he liked about me, Dennis said, "I am ready to pursue a relationship with you."

"I don't believe you. I've heard this before," I replied.

He repeated himself several times and due to my resistance, finally shared this word picture with me.

"It's as if I've been in a boat on a lake for the past several years and though there have been other women on the lake in boats as well, the fog has thickly veiled them and I have sat stationary. But with you, the fog has moved away from you, I see you clearly, my oars are in the water, and I'm rowing in your direction," Dennis said with a smile as he held me on the dance floor.

A giant grin spread across my face as I squealed, "Well, let me give you an engine!"

The following Thursday we showed up at the CCC weekly meeting holding hands, which was a big shocker to most of the students involved.

Six weeks later, Dennis knelt down on one knee overlooking the Salt Lake Valley and declared, "Lisa Leilani Halversen, I want to spend the rest of my life with you. Will you marry me?"

Giggling with a smile as wide as my face could possibly stretch—and then some—I exclaimed, "YES!!!!"

11

To Have and to Hold

There are two utterly different forms of religion: one
believes that God will love me if I change; the other
believes that God loves me so that I can change![1]

RICHARD ROHR

*P*lanning my wedding would be one of the greatest cultural shifts imaginable for my parents and me. I had never attended a wedding of a family member because they took place in Mormon Temples, which exclude children, and I had always been a child. I have thirty-nine cousins and the majority have married in the Temple, yet I haven't witnessed one ceremony. I didn't know how to plan a wedding, but my mom is the consummate party planner, and seemed glad to fill the shoes of wedding planner. This was a sacrificial act of love on her part, for I knew that each decision represented the death of her dream of seeing her daughter marry in the Temple one day.

The idea of walking down the aisle at First Presbyterian Church in Salt Lake City delighted me. First Presbyterian literally stands in the shadow of the Mormon Temple. I had met Jesus in the shadows and now was being married in the shadow. I have no problem being the center of attention, so the idea of hundreds of people joining Dennis and me as we shared vows was exhilarating. As far as I was concerned, the more people to celebrate with us the better. And, I couldn't believe I was actually going to marry Dennis Brockman! I was looking forward to sharing our wedding day with so many friends.

On a hot August 6, 1992, Dennis, myself, and our wedding party arrived at the church for our wedding rehearsal. I felt so pretty in my white, fitted dress with royal blue polka dots. Our dear friend, Henry Wells, his wife, Debbie, and daughters, Lindsey and Emily, had driven up from Sacramento so that Henry could officiate our wedding and the family could celebrate with us. Groomsmen had traveled from various states to stand beside Dennis. I was giddy. Dennis was calm. My bridesmaids were two girlfriends and the rest were sisters and cousins. This was their first wedding ceremony to participate in as well. Everyone seemed to be working hard to act like this was normal and okay, except my mom, who is incredibly authentic with her emotions. When she arrived at the church, her face was long, she looked on the edge of tears throughout the rehearsal, and couldn't manage even to pretend that she felt any joy about my fast-approaching ceremony to Dennis in that church.

My parents loved Dennis, and aside from the fact that he wasn't Mormon, they thought he would be a wonderful son to them and husband to me. Even so, it felt like the rehearsal was driving another nail deeper into the coffin that housed my parents' dying dreams. Mom was encompassed by grief. My dad may have been as well, but he was able to compartmentalize his emotions. Near the end of the rehearsal, Dennis and I sat on the front pew of the sanctuary and my parents sat directly behind us. I overheard my mom expressing her angst to my dad, "I can't believe we're paying money for her to get married in this place. It's horrible." My insides froze, and I wanted so badly not to let her words touch me. But that wasn't possible and I absorbed them like a sponge.

We pulled ourselves together emotionally for the rehearsal dinner, which took place in my parents' backyard. My parents were gracious hosts to more than ninety attendees that night. We gave rehearsal dinner a whole new meaning by merging Mormon and Christian wedding cultures and inviting all of our extended family and close friends. My parents graciously celebrated Dennis's and my story and our lives. We topped off the night with a little Hukilau action. My parents lived in Hawaii when I was born. Though we only remained there for eight months after my birth, my parents kept the Hawaiian culture present in our lives throughout my life. And no party was complete without my mom beautifully swaying to the Hukilau while my dad sang as he strummed his guitar.

The next day, I smiled as each one of my bridesmaids walked one-by-one through the large dark wood doors and down the center aisle of First Presbyterian Church. The wedding coordinator closed the doors and beckoned me to my place centered behind them. The doors swung open, the organ belted out *Here Comes the Bride*, and I smiled so wide it felt like my mouth might split open. Dennis Brockman, the man of my dreams, was waiting for me in his white tuxedo at the front of the church. Henry talked about God and His fabulous design for marriage, Kevin Pettit serenaded us with Stephen Curtis Chapman's "I Will Be Here," our unity candle refused to light due to an overflow of wax atop the wick, and Dennis and I exchanged vows before three hundred friends and family members. I felt like I was living a dream.

At the reception, one of the most memorable dances for me was dancing with my older brother. Novicely swaying to the music, he and I reminisced about the day. As we talked about the ceremony, he said to me, "Lis, I actually felt the Spirit during your ceremony. I don't really have a category for that." That would have been the last thing I would have thought he would say. I loved that he was willing to share this with me. He didn't have a category for this because Mormons aren't supposed to feel the Holy Spirit in Presbyterian churches, or any church outside of theirs. As a Mormon girl, it had been unimaginable to me that I would feel God's Spirit in a Protestant church. I love how God showed up at my wedding in the medium my family uses to determine truth. God created some tension, but in the good way. I love how God persistently transcends all of the boxes in which we attempt to house Him. Instead, He meets each one of us where we are and speaks in the frequency familiar to us. God had some fun showing off at my wedding. I loved that I was able to share our ceremony, the most significant ceremony of my life, with as many friends and family members as we desired. I loved that no one was excluded from any part of the festivities, down to my little baby niece. I loved that my dad was allowed to walk me down the aisle and place me on Dennis's arm. I love that we could include people from different faiths and backgrounds in our ceremony. I loved that our wedding was as inclusive as we could possibly make it.

In contrast to my own wedding day, some of the saddest events for me since leaving Mormonism are family weddings. All of my siblings have married in the Mormon Temple. Unlike the inclusiveness we enjoyed at my wedding, only select adult family members who are Temple-worthy are able to be with the bride and groom in the ceremony. Dennis and I and one aunt have been the only ones from the clan who are unworthy to attend the weddings. So, while all of the adults head downtown to the Salt Lake Temple, Dennis and I hang out at my parents' home for a while, then make our way to the Temple grounds for pictures following the ceremony. As the years have grown and my siblings have had children, we have become the wedding sitters. We tend some of the children during the ceremony and then take them to the Temple grounds with us for photos. Mormon Temple weddings have a unique way of minimizing and excluding those deemed unworthy. Once we arrive at the Temple, we wait and wander around a bit. We watch as other brides and grooms have their pictures taken on the Temple steps, surrounded by their families. At the Salt Lake Temple, it seems as though there is a daily assembly line of brides and grooms. Thus, while we wait for our family to exit the building, we are surrounded by other couples having their pictures taken. After an hour or more of waiting, our family begins to filter out of the Temple a few at a time. They're sharing little stories from the ceremony and laughing together. We mingle and the feeling of being an unworthy outsider lurks around every corner. Eventually, there is rumor that the bride and groom are preparing to exit the building. We form a human corridor for them to walk through and scream as they open the doors. The last time we saw them, they were unmarried. Now they are husband and wife, and we weren't able to witness that evolution due to our unworthiness. Thankfully, I have had Dennis's companionship through all of my siblings' weddings. I didn't realize how much moral support being with each other outside the Temple provided for me until two years ago.

It was the day of my lovely niece's wedding. She was the first of my nieces or nephews to marry and we share a unique connection. I flew to Utah without Dennis for this event because he needed to stay in Orlando with our kids who were in school. I drove downtown to the Temple grounds alone, leaving an hour after everyone else had departed for the wedding ceremony. I was broadsided by the loneliness encompassing me as I walked through the gate to the Temple grounds that beautiful May day. The grounds were fairly unpopulated, as it was mid-week. I walked toward the place where the bride and groom would exit as a married couple following the ceremony and searched for a sunny spot to sit while I waited. There weren't many options available to me so I sat down on a foot-high embankment surrounding a garden. The ache of loneliness settled in my heart. There I sat in the shadow of the Temple with Jesus, unable to be part of the most significant ceremony my niece will experience in her life. I texted my sister-in-law who has also left the Church to invite another who understands into my loneliness. As people passed me by, I wondered what they thought about me, the obvious outsider who is dressed in her Sunday best and waiting for the worthy to exit the holy place so that she may be with them again.

Forty-five minutes after I arrived, my unmarried niece joined me in the shadows. There was something anchoring about having the companionship of someone else in that space. We bantered, laughed, and waited together. Though it cured some of the loneliness, the ache remained.

About ninety minutes after my arrival, family members slowly filtered out of the Temple. Twenty minutes later, the bride and groom threw open the glass double doors and walked out as husband and wife. As we mingled and awaited the time to pose for photos, I overheard people referencing funny parts of the ceremony and laughing with each other. I asked them to share what they were laughing about, and they attempted to capture it—but you really needed to be there. I thought about how I tend to be with a large group of family, many of whom are incredibly sensitive to making sure people don't feel left out of the circle. In fact, my mom and dad are some of the most intentional includers I know. Every major holiday, our family is joined by at least twenty people whom my parents have adopted as family. They might be considered outsiders in other spaces, but not in the Halversen home.

In contrast, when a family member leaves the Mormon Church, that same sensitivity is not extended to them. The mentality is, "Lisa's left the Church, and this is one of her consequences," or perhaps they just don't think about the inherent exclusivity of the whole enterprise. Many aspects of Mormon culture shame apostates. For me, Mormon weddings pack the greatest punch. I love my people and want to celebrate with them, but in that significant life event, I'm reminded that I'm still unworthy according to their doctrine and must remain on the outside of the circle during one of the most important life events for us all.

Shame is difficult to shed. It seems to prowl in unobserved crevices of the soul, coming out to play when the circumstances are just right to accuse the carrier that they are bad. Mormonism is replete with external standards that determine worthiness and unworthiness. Worthiness means someone is meeting all of these external criteria, unworthiness means they've failed to meet them, and the result is shame—they're unworthy of God's presence.

As I grew more acquainted with Jesus, the dualistic beliefs and thinking I possessed were severely challenged. Mormonism equipped me with so many categories that enabled me to judge swiftly whether or not something was right or wrong—in myself and in others. As I read about Jesus, I discovered that He continually pushed back on the dualistic thinking of the religious people of His day and pushed them into mystery where love can flourish. For example, He was not put off by people consuming alcohol, but actually was accused of being a wine bibber Himself. As a Mormon, I was taught that wine wasn't made with the same strength back in Jesus's time as it is today so when the Bible talked about Him drinking wine, it didn't have the same effect on people as now. This is how we reconciled the fact that our Word of Wisdom banned the consumption of alcohol even though Jesus drank it. I began to see that Jesus was the embodiment of edgy—He pushed the envelope. He did not condemn the woman seeking life in many different men, but strategically placed Himself where He would be present *with her.* Upon encountering her, He did not condemn her, but called her spade a spade (adultery—see John 4) and offered her Himself instead, for He alone knew what would truly satisfy her soul's thirst. He provoked the religious, law-upholding men on the Sabbath by breaking it right before their eyes. Then He rebuked them for how their religiosity was impeding a life of love. "The Sabbath was made for man, not man for the Sabbath" (Mark 2:27).

> God persistently transcends all of the boxes in which we attempt to house Him. Instead, He meets each one of us where we are and speaks in the frequency familiar to us.

That's the kind of God He is. He's the God who thrusts people into mystery of His love where there is room to create, to breathe easy, to test the waters, to question, to challenge, to doubt, to shake a fist, and to weep.

All of the external standards the religious people used to determine their goodness and worthiness created an arrogant, righteous inner circle and excluded those who failed to uphold their laws, deeming them unworthy. It was so mind-boggling that Jesus took all of my shame onto Himself on the cross—absorbing it into Himself so that

I no longer needed to wear it—that it took me almost a year to accept His gift of eternal life. However, once I did receive His love, His grace released me into a life of freedom from the laws of men. I was free to relate to God and enjoy His presence whenever and wherever I happened to be. He was free to relate to me no matter how dark I may be at any given moment. In fact, He delighted in shining the light of His love into my darkness, because He knew how intimacy with Him would transform me. His love offered me freedom to navigate a life that delighted and honored Him, and this freedom stirred my love for Him. He had renamed me *beloved and worthy* because of His sacrifice for me and was remaking me through a life of love rather than rules.

Jesus summed up the law of God with two sentences when He was asked, "[Jesus], which is the greatest commandment in the law?"

Jesus replied: "'Love the Lord your God with all your heart and with all your soul and with all your mind.' This is the first and greatest commandment. And the second is like it: 'Love your neighbor as yourself.' All the Law and the Prophets hang on these two commandments" (Matthew 22:36-40 NIV).

I had been loved extravagantly and was created to release His love back to Him and pour it into others. His grace freed me to live this kind of life. His law nurtured a life of love and released my soul from the chains of legalism. The reality that His law was all about love has taken twenty-seven years to sink into the cracks and crevices in my soul where the Mormon doctrine of a conditionally loving God who hangs me out to dry when I fail has sought to remain rooted. Slowly but surely, Jesus reminds me that His love will not exclude me from His presence but will faithfully encompass me. I have the ability to hinder our closeness through the way I live my life and the choices I make moment by moment. I could move away from Him and tell Him to go away. He would honor my desires, for He is love and love does not force itself on another. However, I am always included in the circle of love of the Father, Son, and Holy Spirit, and He is intensely eager to be as involved in my life as I desire. He is a relentless pursuer. It has taken time for these realities to embed themselves in the soil of my heart, mind, body, and spirit. As they have woven their way through my life's tapestry, it has created a vivid contrast to the shame-inducing culture that formed me throughout the first part of my life.

Dennis and I moved to Orlando a year after we were married, and that was good for me. The distance gave me distance from the parts of Mormon culture that made it challenging for me to live in Salt Lake City. I think it also gave my relationship with my parents some breathing room after a tumultuous eighteen months. We had fought hard for our relationship and had taken plenty of blows, and the physical distance between us provided space to heal. We shared a deep affection, so I missed my family immensely, but I also enjoyed the space to exhale and not be confronted by Mormon culture on a moment by moment basis. Some of the culture was life-giving and some of it felt like a wet blanket stealing my breath. In Orlando, I wasn't reminded every Sunday that I was the black sheep of the family. Of course, even in Utah it wasn't necessarily a family member who would cause me to feel that way, but the voices in my head. I had been so successfully indoctrinated that the Mormon voices of judgment would play like a tape in my head when I was with the people I loved.

You are the apostate who wrecked the eternal family.

And then I'd hear the voices of others.

She didn't search with a genuine heart; otherwise, she would still have a testimony that the Church is true.

She just doesn't understand the gospel.

She left the Church because she wanted to drink coffee and tea.

Gary fed her a bunch of lies and she just believed it all.

She dresses so immodestly, wearing those tank tops and short shorts.

How sacrilegious that she wears a cross!

I was free of those voices of shame in Orlando. However, each time I returned to Utah to visit family they haunted me. They are dark, condescending voices that don't consider how greatly it costs a Mormon to leave her faith. I haven't met a post-Mormon who apostatizes flippantly. Yet these voices trivialize the decision to leave and don't respect that extensive thought and seeking to understand history and doctrine that often give a Mormon the courage to leave his or her faith and culture. It costs everything, but the voices of shame and dualistic thinking don't have a paradigm to consider the costs of another. They're happy to sit in a posture of judgment and contempt. In Orlando, those voices lost their power and helped me to rest from the noise of them.

Tank Tops, Coffee, and Tea

It's kind of funny when wearing a tank top and short shorts as a married woman or drinking coffee and tea feels recklessly scandalous. Words cannot describe how incredibly relieved I was not to have to wear Mormon underwear throughout my adult life! As a child, I wanted the protection I was told they would bring, but as a young woman, they lost their appeal. Though I had dreamed of marrying in the Temple, the dreaded reality that accompanied the wedding would be the requirement to wear homely underwear, which provided forced modesty. In summertime when it is blazing hot, wearing an extra layer felt suffocating to me. In addition, my shorts would have needed to drop close to my knees, and no sleeveless tops would be allowed in order to cover the garments. As I folded my parents' holy underwear on laundry day throughout my girlhood, it was difficult to stomach the idea that one day I would be covered in them myself. I liked Victoria's Secret and pretty undergarments. I thought of the garments in the same way I thought about polygamy in heaven—it's just one of those pills I'll have to swallow.

When I visited Utah during the summertime as a Christ-follower, I embraced the freedom of wearing tank tops and short shorts. But the voices of judgment haunted me for years, even though I no longer believed that the way I dressed made me holy or unholy, worthy or unworthy. I found myself aware that people might be judging me because I was wearing a wedding ring, but not wearing garments. Running into someone from my past would cause this shaming voice to spew acid over me as I imagined what they might be thinking of me.

Why isn't she wearing garments?

I wonder what she did to make herself unworthy of a Temple marriage?

The external standards of holiness wreaked havoc on my mind and it took a great deal of energy to remind myself that I was not unholy because I wore tank tops and short shorts.

I needed to believe this: "I'm okay and God is with me in my tank top and short shorts. Not only is He with me but He delights in me. I am the Temple of the living God and He lives in me, not in buildings (see 1 Corinthians 3:16-17; Acts 17:24). He has found me worthy of living within me because Jesus has made me clean. I'm not immodest, but beautiful and free to dress in a way that honors Him and doesn't require me to wear homely underwear." It was about twelve years after converting to Christianity before I was able to silence these voices of shame and contempt and tune into the kind voice of God.

Another subject that challenged my ability to live freely around my family was the expectation of adherence to the Word of Wisdom. Since leaving Mormonism, I live in the tension between desiring to honor my parents and family and living in the freedom that Jesus affords me.

During the fall of my senior year of college, I was taking eighteen credit hours and completely overwhelmed by the demands of my coursework. I had changed my major from business to communications that year so I needed to ramp up on communication classes. I wasn't a writer and thought communications was all about speaking. Thus, the three five-page essays I had due each Friday were a rude awakening for this novice writer. I stopped by my parents' home one day to use their computer to type an essay. Exhausted from late nights of study and another late night ahead, I had stopped at 7-Eleven to pick up a mocha. This drink wasn't part of my normal routine, but in times of need, it provided the necessary boost to persevere in my studies. I had also been recently diagnosed with fibromyalgia after a long history of athletic injuries from which my body couldn't seem to heal. With my academic demands and health struggles, I showed up at my parents' home with my backpack and mocha in hand.

As I walked into the front entry, my mom came into view. When she saw my thick, paper cup she came toward me and gasped with her entire body. "Is that coffee?!" she exclaimed in horror.

"It's a hot chocolate with some coffee," I said, wanting to explain my plight. But there wasn't time or space to do that. I had brought one of the world's evils into her home and it triggered a massive emotional earthquake. It wasn't honoring to my parents, and I was normally sensitive to that. Perhaps it wouldn't have had the same impact if I was still active in the Mormon Church. Perhaps this cup of mocha was a symbol of my apostasy and it brought all of that emotional pain to the surface. Whatever the reality, it was as if some contained creature broke through the desolation she'd experienced the previous nine months and exploded in force.

"Get that out of my house!" she cried. This small cup of mocha caused my mother to burst with pain and anger like an erupting volcano. I abruptly turned and walked out the front door with my heart practically beating out of my chest. I knew that we were all living on the emotional edge, but I didn't expect the intensity of her reaction. If it was a beer, her reaction would have made sense to me. But for devout Mormons like my parents, beer and coffee were equally horrific vices.

Throughout my teenage years, I was surrounded by Mormons who consumed Coca-Cola products like water. There seemed to be ambiguity to me even in the black and white nature of the Word of Wisdom. Coffee, tea, and alcohol were the evil drinks of the world, but we could consume as much Coca-Cola, Dr Pepper, or Mountain Dew as we desired. I never understood why soda pop, which was filled with corn syrup and a bunch of unhealthy chemicals, was more acceptable to consume than coffee or tea.

For years when my parents visited me in Orlando, I would hide my tea bags and coffee beans. It was a strange tension in me. I wasn't a Mormon anymore and my husband had never been one, so the Mormon Word of Wisdom wasn't looming over us. But, I didn't want to give my family more reasons to judge me than they already had. I also wanted to avoid the emotional fallout that could occur as a result of this cultural/doctrinal difference between us. There were enough of these land mines as it was, so hiding something small like this seemed manageable. It took twenty years before I didn't hide the coffeepot and tea bags when family came to our home to visit. I don't blame my family for that. It just gives a window into how challenging it is to shed the cloak of shame that accompanied my apostasy as well as the desire to reduce as much as possible the presence of land mines that could create tension.

Parts of Mormon culture were life-giving, like the way we all valued family. My parents are so devoted to their children and grandchildren that they host monthly Sunday dinners to bring us together. They take us on entire-family vacations several times each year and enable my family to return to Utah each Christmas so we can be together as a big family unit. My parents take their grandchildren to plays, musicals, and the ballet because they love the arts and love to generously spend time with them and invest in their lives. From the time my kids were born, my mom made sure to come to Orlando and stay with us for at least two weeks each year; she would take such pleasure in throwing parties for the kids. She had in her possession decorations and party-gear to celebrate with us whatever holidays were within three months of her arrival. She loved to help me homeschool my kids and took the initiative to help me around the house in whatever way was needed.

On Sundays, she usually went to the LDS Church by herself while we went to First Presbyterian Church. She also lovingly entered our world some Sundays and joined us for a cross-cultural experience at our church, which was not terribly comfortable for any of us because it brought tension. But she would bravely pose her questions to us to better understand our culture and the doctrine we believe.

My dad has faithfully pursued me through letters and phone calls since we moved twenty-five years ago. There was a season after his retirement when he worked for short two-week stints on the East Coast of the US. He would fly down to stay with us in Orlando over the weekend between weeks. When I shared with our church music director that my dad had sung in the Mormon Tabernacle Choir, she was elated and invited him to join the choir of First Presbyterian Church on the Sundays he was in town. My dad crossed the chasm, donned his choir robe with a cross embroidered at the nape of his neck, and sang with our choir as a guest member whenever he was in town. I deeply appreciate how my parents and family value being with each other and pull out the stops to be together and maintain relationship.

Another aspect of Mormon culture I think is wonderful is the community they create. I have not encountered such a supportive network of people since I departed from the Church. During the month of December, Christmas gifts from neighbors flooded our kitchen. Homemade sweets, breads, and treats faithfully arrived throughout the month. If a person was in need, other members were there with meals and service to care for the struggling member. This might not be every Mormon's reality, but it was my reality.

Elderhood and Authority

In January of 2009, I received a phone call from a woman I know from the church we had attended for eight years. After chatting for a few minutes, she extended to me one of the most surreal invitations I've received in my lifetime.

"Lisa, I'm on the elder nominating committee. We spend time together asking God to lead us to the group of church members whom we nominate for the next class of elders. You are one of the people our committee has decided would make an excellent spiritual leader for our congregation," Cara continued.

My jaw dropped as far as it possibly could extend.

"What exactly is involved in being an elder in our congregation?" I asked, still baffled they had chosen me. Though I had attended First Presbyterian Church of Orlando for eight years, it was such a large church with thousands of members that I didn't feel like I knew very many people very well. It was challenging for me to feel connected there and I felt a bit anonymous at the time.

Cara shared that our church elders are a board of thirty-six people who provide spiritual leadership for our congregation. They are the decision makers and the ruling body of our congregation. In order to be an elder, I would need to complete theological coursework throughout the fall in preparation. If I were to accept the nomination, I would be required to attend a monthly business meeting with all the elders and pastors of the church. In addition, I would join a ministry team and meet with them monthly and execute whatever I would need to do to fulfill my role. I would be on duty once a month, meaning I would need to be on the church campus during all three services on Sundays. I would have the privilege of praying for a person being baptized on behalf of the congregation. All these responsibilities felt like such an honor to me. But there was one more: as an elder, Cara said, I would have the privilege of serving communion to the congregation.

Those words settled into me in a way only an ex-Mormon woman could experience. Cara couldn't have known the weight this carried in my soul. I would have the authority to serve the bread and the cup symbolizing the body and blood of Christ to fellow members of my church body. Mormon women are forever excluded from holding the priesthood, so they only have the opportunity to possess spiritual authority through their husbands. I definitely wouldn't ever be serving the sacrament. As I considered whether or not to accept the invitation to be ordained an elder in our church, I thought of the contrast between the position of elder in Christian churches and the Mormon Church. The thought of twelve-year-old boys serving communion to my congregation was unconscionable. One of the stunning realities of being in relationship with the biblical God is that all of His followers hold the priesthood, men and women alike (1 Peter 2:9).

Dennis and I decided it would be an honor for me to serve our congregation as an elder. Dennis was so proud of me and celebrated who God has made me to be as a spiritual leader. Dennis wasn't threatened by the offer and wanted me to flourish in the roles God brought my way. In January 2009, I was asked to come to the front of First Presbyterian Church's opera-hall-like sanctuary alongside the other eleven men and women who had also been elected. We were asked to kneel before our congregation. Our church's college of elders was asked to come forward, surround us, and lay hands on us as we were ordained into the office of elder. Kneeling in that place, surrounded by other elders and covered by their hands, was one of the most surreal moments of my life. To worship in a place that believes that the image of God is more completely represented when men and women are both at the table of leadership is an immeasurable gift.

A month later, my first opportunity to serve communion arrived. I stood at the front of the sanctuary with the bread on a large plate in my hands. Next to me was a man holding a large chalice full of grape juice. As music played, the congregation lined up and began partaking of this feast of remembrance. Before long, the people I couldn't wait to serve walked toward me. One by one, I was honored to serve my kids.

"Madison, the body of Christ broken for you. Keegan, the body of Christ broken for you. Cole, the body of Christ, broken for you." They smiled as they looked in my eyes and tore off a chunk of bread. I could tell they were proud of their momma. Behind them was Dennis. A grin lit up his face as he came near.

"Dennis, the body of Christ, broken for you," I said affectionately. He tore off a chunk of bread while looking into my eyes then moved to the elder standing beside me to dip his chunk of bread in the grape juice. This was a surreal experience and one that I will never take for granted.

I was apprehensive to share with my parents that I had been ordained as an elder in my church. I didn't know what to expect and I always felt cautious about topics that resided in the cultural expanse between our beliefs. But when I finally shared the news with them, I could hear the smiles spread across their faces through the phone. They sounded like proud parents. They respect my relationship with

God and celebrate who He's made me to be. Last Christmas, as I sat with my parents and sister around the dining table at Snowbird, Utah, I shared with them some of the doors God has been opening for me to teach and pour my life into others. They were excited for me and proud of me. They asked me questions with wonderful curiosity and I shared about my fear that I don't have the resources to rise to the challenges these opportunities will present.

After a life-giving hour, my mom—spilling forth tears—offered this to me, "Lisa, I'm flashing back to a needlepoint you made when you were eight years old that said, 'I will follow Heavenly Father's plan for me.' When you left the Church, I didn't believe you were following His plan for you. I thought you were way out of His plan and I was torn up over it. But as you've lived your life over the years and I see where He's taken you and the opportunities you've been given to influence others with His love, I see that you have been in the center of His plan all along. He needed to take you outside of the Church to do this because His plans for you couldn't have been accomplished in the Church. They were far more expansive."

> We have learned to love in the middle place, where black and white could not survive.

I sat there, hand in hand with my mom, staring into both of my parents' eyes, stunned by her words. Tears rolled down my cheeks. We have learned to love in the middle place, where black and white could not survive. The rigidity of clear lines has died a very slow death, but their painful crucifixion has given birth to mystery. And mystery has given birth to life. We have all had to die to dreams. We have lived in the tension of departing to different churches on Sundays when we are together, as well as the sacrifice and discomfort of occasionally visiting one another's churches. We have lived in the tension of knowing we don't share the same essential beliefs and the discomfort that reality creates. We have lived in the tension of accommodating each other's cultures and spiritual dialect. We have navigated the tension of awkward and uncomfortable doctrinal conversations, hoping to understand each other better. We have journeyed through the wide expanse of chaos and storm, of uncertainty and hopelessness, of ache and eventual expectancy. We have all battled hard to land in this soft place where love resides.

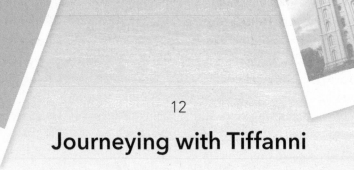

12

Journeying with Tiffanni

When brokenness is disdained, where the real story is never
told, the power of God is not felt. Where brokenness is invited
and received with grace, the gospel comes alive with hope.[1]

LARRY CRABB

This past winter, my daughter walked through the front door after
school one day and declared, "There's a family from Utah who
moved into a house down the street. They have a son in my grade." I
couldn't believe it—I hadn't had the pleasure of a living near a neighbor from Utah since we moved to Orlando twenty-seven years ago. I
was excited to meet this family. Just the thought of having a neighbor
who has shared in the experience of living in Utah culture was exciting.

The following week as I turned into our subdivision, I saw a tall,
blond woman standing outside of the "Utah family house." I pulled
my Excursion in front of her home, rolled down the window, and in
a refined manner, yelled to her across my truck, "I'm Lisa. My daughter says you're from Utah, is that right?"

"Yep. We are. I'm Tiffanni."

Immediately I felt our connection. She was warm, bubbly and a
Utah accent tinged her words.

"I'm so happy to meet you and would love to have you over for
lunch!" I said.

"I would love to have lunch with you." Tiffanni excitedly replied.

"Fabulous. Are you Mormons?" I asked, wanting to know if they had a Word of Wisdom to accommodate.

"Yes, we are. Are you?" Tiffanni asked.

"No, we aren't," I replied. "But I'll be sure to have some sparkling water instead of iced tea then." (It's a Southern thing.)

With that short introduction, Tiffanni already felt like a sister to me. We shared an immediate connection and mutual affection.

As I prepared lunch for us four days after our introduction, I was thinking how surreal it was to have a new Mormon neighbor move here from Utah. God pretty much blew my mind. I was hoping that my relationship with Tiffanni would be one where I would get to love on her with Jesus's love for a lot of years, and pray for God to open the door for us to be able to talk about our doctrinal beliefs with each other. When a Mormon is devout in his/her beliefs and armed with his/her default mantras, doctrinal conversations can be futile and frustrating for everyone. When Jesus prayed for His followers before He went to the cross, He told them that people would know they follow Him by their love for each other (John 13:35). I assumed Tiffanni's and my friendship would be absent of conversation about our faiths for at least a while, but filled with huge doses of love. My assumptions were so wrong.

We had Tiffanni's family over for dinner that weekend and bonded over volleyball, burgers, and my son's card tricks, as well as his bearded dragon, Finn. We were elated to finally have neighbors who felt like family to us. Five days later, Tiffanni came for another lunch. She walked into our home freely sharing with me the difficulties each of her family members has faced in their transition to Orlando. They were all in culture shock. Their small Utah town had felt like living in Mayberry,[2] and had provided a sheltered environment for their kids. Orlando had brought with it a level of exposure to the world's value system that represented a loss for them. Tiffanni vulnerably shared her struggles with me, and I was privileged to be with her in that place, holding her angst and regret. We took our Caesar salads out to the back porch and as we sat down Tiffanni boldly asked me, "So what's your story? Were you ever a Mormon?" I was so grateful for her candor and curiosity. It opened the door of our friendship to honest dialogue.

"Yes, I grew up in a Mormon family in Salt Lake City. I believed the Church was true with all of my heart throughout my childhood—never doubted that," I shared. I told her about meeting Gary, and how he challenged me to defend my faith. I told her how disillusioned I was to find that my way of "knowing the Church was true" through a burning in my bosom wasn't enough for me when my beliefs were confronted. I told her about my secretive search and the disillusionment that had haunted me throughout that year as I uncovered disheartening realities about Mormon history, Joseph Smith's character and lifestyle, and most importantly the conflicting Mormon and biblical plans of salvation. I sought to be gentle and honest in telling my story.

Tiffanni interrupted me, "I cannot believe you are my neighbor! I converted to the Church at nineteen years old, served a mission, have believed in it undoubtingly since joining, have served in my callings faithfully, and lived Temple-worthy. Then a year ago, I began reading the *Essays,* which Church leaders have been encouraging the members to read on the Church website."

These *Gospel Doctrine Essays* were about the history of the Mormon Church and Joseph Smith. While reading the *Essays,* Tiffanni learned disturbing historical inaccuracies regarding what she had been taught about Joseph Smith. She had always known that the early Church practiced polygamy, but she had been taught that it was mainly done because there were more women than men. In order to provide more effectively, the men took on more than one wife. She'd taught people that very lesson during her own mission. But the *Essays* made it clear that Joseph had married over 30 wives—and many of them were already married to other men. This was polyandry, not just polygamy.

It also disturbed Tiffanni that Joseph Smith had claimed to have had a vision that he was to take a fourteen-year-old girl as one of his new wives. He insisted to the girl's father that he had had a vision that an angel stood over him with a flaming sword, commanding him to do this. Even for the standards of the late 1800s, this was too young. "In our church," said Tiffanni, "the most important value we hold is that of free agency. Where is the free agency in Joseph Smith telling a fourteen-year-old girl her salvation is dependent upon her willingness to comply with his vision and marry him?" The *Essays* also revealed that during the time of the prophet's polyandry, he sent specific men on missions, and then had their wives sealed to him without the husband's knowledge.

Tiffanni continued, "I know a prophet is just a man and that he's not perfect, but I couldn't accept that this was from God. I didn't know if I could support a church based on the vision of a 'Prophet' who did this. It was such a blast of a paradigm shift—I've been a mess the past year." Tiffanni said she also felt betrayed. Why had she never been taught this? She was encouraged to study the words and lives of the modern-day prophets along with the ancient prophets. So why hadn't these uncomfortable truths been mentioned before now? Tiffanni said she had believed in the Church with all her heart and sacrificed so much of herself to be a good, faithful member. Now, she felt tilted off her axis. "I don't know what to do. I believe Joseph Smith is a true prophet, but I can't reconcile this information about him, and it was the Church leaders who encouraged me to read about it," Tiff continued.

"Tiffanni, be gracious with yourself. You're in major transition having just moved here and your spiritual world feels like it's falling apart," I offered. She sighed deeply.

"We still go to church," she said, "but I cannot believe it anymore. The trouble with Mormonism is that if you don't believe it completely, it all falls apart. But I am also struggling with the thought that God is punishing me as a result of my doubts. I feel completely disoriented."

This was true to Mormon theology and, though I wasn't surprised to hear this come out of Tiff's mouth, it broke my heart.

"Why would God punish you?" I asked.

Tiffanni replied, "My husband and I were having doubts about our religion before we moved, and I wondered if Heavenly Father had withdrawn His presence from us because we're not worthy of the Spirit as a result of our doubts."

My heart now bleeding for her, I shared, "The biblical God doesn't work that way. He welcomes your doubts and questions."

"What do you mean the *biblical* God?" Tiffanni asked. "Everyone worships the same God. We have different paths to God, but they all lead to God."

"I believed that when I was a Mormon as well," I said. "But as I studied the Bible, I came to see that the biblical God is incredibly specific about His identity and voicing to His people that His identity matters. He makes clear distinctions between Himself and all of the other gods people worship, making clear that He is the only true God."

I could tell by Tiffanni's body language that this was a new idea to her and she wasn't buying it.

"Tiffanni, think about this illustration and the importance of identity. There's a woman named Tiffanni who has three children and lives in East Orlando. She married in the Mormon Temple and moved to Orlando this year. There's another woman named Tiffanni. She is a single woman and a prostitute. She doesn't have any children and lives in downtown Orlando. These women share the same name. Is it possible for those two women to be the same person?" I asked.

"Well, they could be," Tiffanni replied.

"How could they be? They're completely different people." Tiffanni resisted this foreign idea. She sat quietly in my sun-soaked screened porch, forming her response. I could see the resistance to want to admit to this.

"Hmm, I guess they can't really be the same person." Tiffanni conceded with some hesitation. "But we believe in the same Jesus, who was born in Nazareth and performed miracles and died for our sins"

"God is clear throughout the Bible that He is the only true God, unchanging, and has always been and always will be God," I said. "The Mormon god is flesh and bones and exalted into godhood through making his nature one that changes. But John 4:24 says that God the Father is Spirit, not flesh and bones."

Tiffanni was working hard to understand this new paradigm of thinking about God. I was completely shocked that we were freely having this conversation during our first lunch date. Usually it takes years of being in relationship with a Mormon before we venture into these waters. I paused to let this new concept of the importance of God's identity settle into her.

I gently asked Tiffanni, "How can an unchanging, all-knowing, all-powerful God who formed us and created us to participate in His life of love, and claims to be the only true God, be the same God as one who was once a man, married to Heavenly Mother, progressed into godhood, and whose offspring have the potential to exalt into godhood like He did? They are two completely different identities."

I remembered when Gary had challenged me to consider this same topic and felt compassion for my new friend. Her world already felt like it was spinning out of control and I wanted to offer her a life-line in the biblical Jesus. But I remembered how Gary offering me a lifeline to the biblical Jesus had brought tumultuous waters with it.

Tiffanni didn't have much to offer in response but was deep in thought. It was as if I had walked her through a door that led into a completely foreign land, and she didn't have a paradigm yet for how to absorb the sounds and thinking of this new place. I was privileged to have the opportunity to take her by the hand and lead her through these doors into unknown places. Because I had been in her shoes twenty-eight years earlier, compassion and empathy energized my words. I was sensitive to how each concept would land on her, and was asking God to tune me into His heart for Tiffanni as we conversed. She was staying open to me, and still curious, as she wrestled through these concepts of identity.

"It took me ten months of wrestling with this concept before I saw the importance of it," I said gently. "If you think about it, our view of God affects everything about us. It affects how we see Him and how we see others. If our view of God is that He requires obedience to certain laws in order to be worthy of His love and presence, then we relate to Him under conditions—either striving to be worthy enough, or growing weary and indifferent to God's transactional love and giving up. I find it important to note that we take precautions to protect our identities, because who we are matters. If somebody steals our identity, it costs us severely. So, why is the identity of God any different?"

I paused and refilled Tiffanni's cup with water. I knew this was heavy for our first lunch, but this is where the conversation naturally flowed and I was responding to her invitation to keep talking about hard subjects.

I told Tiffanni how I had carried my view of the Mormon god into my life with the biblical God, and that it had taken years to remove these ways of thinking from my relationship with Him. I would find myself fearing that God was going to "hang me out to dry," I said. "That isn't the identity of the biblical God who never forsakes His people, but after spending the first eighteen years of my life believing that God leaves me when I'm not worthy of His presence, it was challenging to not believe that the biblical God would relate to me in the same way."

"I am definitely feeling unworthy of God's Spirit right now, just because of my doubts." Tiffanni was shaking her head. "I shouldn't feel that way just for asking questions." For a moment she saw the craziness of her reality.

"According to the biblical God, we're all unworthy," I said. "We can't make ourselves worthy enough to meet His perfect standard of love. The Bible teaches that Adam and Eve's sin infected their children and every generation thereafter. Mormon doctrine teaches that people have a divine nature, whereas the Bible teaches that people possess a sinful nature. This basically means that, by nature, we are inclined to make ourselves, other people, or created things the axis around which our lives spin rather than God. God created us to live with Him forever in His community of perfect love. Because of sin, we look for life outside of Him. And we can't do enough to pay the price for our sins. So, God the Father sent God the Son to this earth, taking on skin and bones, to show us how to love Him and each other, and to give us a vision of what it looks like to live in His kingdom. His time on earth culminated in Jesus sacrificing Himself in our place, becoming sin for us, and absorbing the cost of our sin, which is death and separation from doing life with Him. Only a perfect sacrifice could satisfy God's perfect law of love. God (the Father) gave God (the Son) to defeat the idolatry in our hearts and evil in this world. Through Jesus, we are made worthy of eternal life. No amount of good works has the ability to change your nature. But when you accept that Jesus died for you and invite Him into your life, He cuts away your sinful nature and infuses you with a new nature—His divine nature (2 Peter 1:3-4). You are made righteous and worthy through Christ alone."

Tiffanni was focused and thoughtful, "This is another paradigm shift, but there is something about it that makes sense to me. I never feel like I'm enough. As faithful a Mormon as I have been, obeying the laws and ordinances of the gospel, I am still always falling short. I am constantly repenting and trying to do better, to feel worthy, yet I never quite feel like I am enough."

We let this settle for a bit. Though we were in the middle of winter in Orlando, it was a lovely sunny day, and as the sun's rays shone onto Tiffanni's face, I saw Jesus's light lifting her heavy soul. She was in the depths, in the fiercest spiritual battle of her adult life, and it had taken a toll on her. Our conversation was like a cup of cold water for both of us.

Tiffanni exclaimed, "I can't believe you're my neighbor. What are the odds of me moving down the street from you? I knew when I met you there was something different about you and the Spirit was alive and strong in you. I have no doubt that Heavenly Father brought us together. My husband read and researched the *Essays* first and questioned the veracity of the Church five years ago. He didn't tell me, and he kept going to church with us all those years. He learned how to avoid church callings,[3] and has kept taking his family to church in spite of his doubt. He's continued his activity in the Church based on duty and a desire to teach the kids a sense of morality."

I could understand her husband's journey, but I ached for him. The torture of navigating hidden waters and wearing a mask is tiring. But it is often the price a Mormon spouse who's questioning his faith must pay in order to keep his marriage intact.

"How has he kept going all of these years?" I asked.

"He is one of the most loyal people I've ever met. He doesn't want his kids to be ostracized—which they would have been in Utah—and he didn't want to lose our marriage. But he is so disillusioned by the Church that he's questioning the existence of God."

"I totally understand, Tiffanni. There is so much at stake in leaving the Church. I'm so thankful my eyes were opened to the reality of the LDS Church before I married and had children. I can't imagine navigating these waters married and with kids."

"We went to a counselor before leaving Utah because this was tearing us up. We wanted counsel about whether or not he should tell his family about his doubts and live honestly. The counselor told us not to tell his parents, because his mom might not recover from the news. I'm so grateful I can talk about this with you. You are the only person in my life I can be completely honest with about all of my wrestling and doubts."

I shared her affection. Being neighbors felt like a gift from God—that He brought us together at this time in our lives—while I was writing this book and she was in the terrifying process of researching and questioning her religion. Lunch had lasted three hours, and a phone call from her daughter awakened us to the reality that kids were returning from school, and that we needed to leave behind this unique space. We embraced as she walked out the door, eager to be with each other again.

Wanna Go on a Walk?

The following week, I was heading out for an evening walk and stopped by to see if Tiffanni would like to join me. Excitedly, she stepped into her running shoes and we were off. I was so happy to have some time to get to know better this new friend whom I felt like I had known my entire life. For the next hour, as we walked around our neighborhood, Tiffanni shared some of her story with me. Her story was so different from my own. She grew up in a broken home with a significant number of stressful transitions throughout her childhood. Her grandparents were the one grounding force in her life. During a season when she lived with them in her early childhood, she attended their Southern Baptist Church.

Amidst the chaos of her teenage years, she began dating a Mormon boy. Though he wasn't tremendously passionate about his faith at the time, his parents were. She loved being in their home, where his mom was loving and present, preparing meals and caring for the family. She saw that the Church brought order to their lives, and she was drawn to their family values. Over time, she met with LDS missionaries for what the Church refers to as *the missionary discussions.* At nineteen, she was baptized a member of the Mormon Church and, being the passionate woman that she is, decided to serve a mission at a time when it was less common for young women to serve missions than it is today.

After her mission, she attended Brigham Young University, and eventually married her husband in the Temple. They had raised their kids in the Church, a reality that added to her angst. Her questioning did not only affect her, but would profoundly affect her children's lives as well. It's difficult enough to muster the courage to leave the Church when single. Figuring out how to tell your kids the religion you've raised them in (and adamantly told them is true a thousand times over) is not really true is an incredibly overwhelming prospect.

As Tiffanni and I rounded the corner onto our street, her children were outside in the dark awaiting our arrival. There is an innocence about them, having lived in a sheltered Utah town for the past five years.

Over the next several weeks, Tiffanni invited our family for dinner, we hosted a movie night for our families, and we all enjoyed spending time together. Tiffanni's family wondered why we were being so nice to them, and we were so happy to have friends who felt like family five houses down the street. This was a rare gift.

One night, I dropped in on them after dinner and Tiffanni was in bed, emotionally crashed. She felt on the edge of hopeless much of the time because of her crisis of faith. We talked for a few minutes and then Tiffanni jumped out of bed, put on her running shoes, and said, "C'mon, let's go for a walk."

Around the Block

We circled our block in the dark, over and over again, as Tiffanni invited me into her angst. "I feel so much shame for not taking my daughter to seminary in the mornings. Getting her to seminary is so hard here. I took for granted that she attended seminary as a class period in Utah. I forced myself out of bed at 4:30 in the morning for the first few months after we moved here. I'm not a morning person, and my daughter has a chronic condition that makes her so uncomfortable at night that she's unable to fall asleep until the wee hours of the morning. So, waking up at 4:30 for both of us was torture. I feel so much shame that I can't be the faithful Mormon mom, pull it together, get out of bed, and sit in that parking lot from 5:30–6:15 a.m. so that my daughter can faithfully attend seminary."

> I'm so weak and this weakness feels like sin to me.

Tiffanni inhaled deeply and then let out an enormous sigh. She does this frequently—it's an attempt to catch a breath while exhaling her stress, fear, and angst.

Tiffanni continued, "I'm so weak and this weakness feels like sin to me. I feel unworthy of the gospel. I am never going to be enough if I can't force myself out of bed in the morning and take my child to seminary."

Her words pierced my heart. I remember all too well the desire to be worthy of the Holy Ghost's presence and guidance, but seeming to fall short much of the time.

"Tiffanni, the upside-down reality of the biblical story is that there is nothing we could possibly do to make ourselves worthy of God's love and presence. Several years ago, as I was overcome with feelings of not being lovable, a mentor of mine looked deep into my eyes and said, 'Isn't it interesting that until we realize how completely unlovable we are, we can't begin to receive an inkling of God's grace?' That response was so unexpected, all I could do was cock my head in bewilderment. I was speechless—that's not a frequent occurrence! Something in me thought I needed to fix this issue so that I could feel lovable. But my mentor turned that idea on its head. He said, 'We aren't lovable, Lisa. We continually turn away from God and look for life outside of Him. And God pursues us and loves us in spite of ourselves. He knew we couldn't make ourselves worthy, so He did it for us. Nothing matters more to Him than being able to envelop us in His love, and restore us into the people He designed us to be, with Him at our center.'"

With curiosity and a tinge of hope in her voice, Tiffanni responded, "Yes! That has to be true. I can't do enough, and I can't be enough to be worthy. But Jesus is enough. Only Jesus is enough."

I was elated and caught by surprise when Tiffanni embraced the biblical realities I shared with her. They were foreign to her, but I could see relief overcome her entire body as their truth sunk into her.

"Tiffanni, listen to how cool this gets. When you place your trust in Christ and respond to His invitation to receive Him, He pours His Spirit into you, filling you to overflowing with His love, and clothing you in His righteousness. When the Father looks on you, He only sees the righteousness of His Son, whose righteousness makes you worthy of being in His presence forever. Here's a word picture that helps capture this reality: as a Mormon, I believed that when I died, I would come to Heavenly Father clothed in my righteous works—my payment of full tithes, active church attendance, service, faithful fulfillment of my church callings, history of obeying the Word of Wisdom, and ultimately, my Temple marriage. Whatever I failed to accomplish in making myself worthy of eternal life, Jesus would make up the difference. I might only need Him to be my socks and shoes, because I would have mostly covered the bases. I would be rewarded and exalted into a goddess, and then would birth spirit babies throughout eternity. I would be married to my husband, who would have been equally faithful and would be a god. This is the picture that captures the essence of Mormon doctrine. Does that sound right to you?"

"Yep, that sounds right to me."

I continued with the illustration, "According to historical, biblical Christianity, salvation and eternal life are one and the same. Salvation does not simply mean the ability to resurrect from the grave. It is eternal life. Ephesians 2:8-9 (NIV) says, 'For it is by grace you have been saved, through faith—and this is not from yourselves, it is the gift of God—not by works, so that no one can boast.' According to the Bible, when we die, we come to God the Father completely clothed in Christ's righteousness. None of our good works could make us worthy of His presence or life in His kingdom. The Bible says we will be rewarded for our works, but those works have nothing to do with how we gain access to eternal life with God. The Father knows His followers because they have been living in His kingdom since they had accepted the reality that they needed a Savior and placed their trust in Jesus Christ's death as payment for their sins. He knows His people and welcomes them into His kingdom based solely on His Son's righteousness."

Tiffanni paused, "That picture makes sense to me. When I was twelve years old, I was watching a Billy Graham Crusade on TV and I asked Jesus into my heart as I was guided through a prayer. I wanted Him in my life! I wanted to know God. Are you saying that on that day, God clothed me in Christ's righteousness, making me worthy to enter into relationship with Him?"

"Yes, if you genuinely placed your faith in Christ that day."

Tiffanni responded swiftly, "I did receive Him! I wanted Him in my life. I've always wanted Him in my life. I need Him in my life."

"Then He clothed you in His righteousness and made you worthy of relationship with Him."

We decided to keep lapping around our block as more and more questions and concerns came to the surface.

"But, if there weren't requirements for me to acquire eternal life, I don't think I would do anything for God. I think I would be lazy and need the requirement of obeying His commands to motivate me," said Tiffanni.

"I used to think like that, too. I didn't have a paradigm that included this kind of transformative grace. I couldn't comprehend that eternal life was a free gift of God that I didn't need to earn in some way. Then I encountered the love of the biblical God. The love of the biblical Jesus is so compelling that it moved me to give up everything to follow Him. As He enveloped me in His love, I desired to love Him back and follow Him wherever He was going. Obedience is no longer required for eternal life, but is a response to Jesus's invitation to deeper intimacy in my relationship with Him. Not only is He my God, but He longs to be my friend. It is a complete paradigm shift, Tiff. You're on a journey, wrestling with the doctrines of your religion. There is dissonance on this path. I think it is helpful to see that God is a lover, who created you for a relationship with Him. He didn't create you for religion."

Her wheels were spinning as we rounded another corner in the dark.

"Yes, He's a relationship!" Tiffanni was seeing and agreeing.

"Religion is man's attempt to bridge the gap between God and people. Religion without relationship puts forth the idea that the burden is on us to bridge that gulf through our works of righteousness. We are supposed to make ourselves worthy, in order to restore relationship with God. We see that in most religions. God's solution to the relational rift between us that comes from our sin is to sacrifice Himself in our place. Jesus bridges the gulf between us and makes us worthy. This is grace. I don't think we can hear it enough, especially when our entire experience of God has been religion without relationship for so many years."

Tiffanni's countenance began to lift a little bit more, and she exclaimed, "That's it! I can see that. Religion is sucking the life out of me, it's killing me. It's done me in."

I was amazed that Tiffanni's eyes were being opened to these realities so swiftly. I was giddy for her and the freedom that Jesus was leading her toward in such a short time since I had met her. I know she had spent a year sitting in her questions and fear, which is a long time. At the same time, she was getting these biblical concepts, and I saw buds of hope sprouting from her weary heart. Buds of hope that this darkness wouldn't last forever as we took each step around our block.

"One of my favorite Bible verses says, 'It is for freedom that Christ has set us free. Stand firm, then, and do not let yourselves be burdened again by a yoke of slavery' (Galatians 5:1 NIV). In its attempt to restore people to God, religion offers a yoke of slavery, because the burden is on us to make ourselves worthy. Relationship with God offers freedom, because we are yoked to Jesus who made us worthy."

"Freedom! I want to live in freedom," Tiffanni exclaimed through another one of her deep sighs. "Jesus came to set us free. Mormonism is not offering me freedom."

Had Tiffanni been the devout, unquestioning Mormon woman that she was for the previous twenty years, I don't think that she would have seen as vividly how the Mormon law was not offering her freedom. It took her coming to a place where she wasn't "pulling it off" in her callings and beliefs to help her see how religion was sucking the life out of her.

"Tiffanni," I said, "Jesus tells us to live in community with others who follow Him and want to grow in relationship with Him. He calls His followers His Church. And He says that there will be unique blessings of His presence when we get together with each other for worship. So, we gather together in worship, but our purpose for doing so is not to become worthy or be approved by God, but to deepen our relationship with Him in community with others who love Him too."

Exhaling her stress, Tiffanni groaned, "Lisa, I don't know what to do. How do I do this? I feel like my soul is a dark, black hole with crusted edges." The costs of her journey would hit her like a two-by-four in the middle of our conversations.

"Tiffanni, you've lived the past twenty-four years with the Mormon Church and its teachings as the axis for your life. It has been everything to you—the paradigm through which you viewed the world and how it works. It has given you a community, a culture, and a structure. You encountered goodness in the Church along with the doctrine that didn't lead you into freedom. It has been the foundation for how you live. It has formed your entire value system. It's no wonder you feel like your soul is a black hole with crusting edges. Your foundation has turned to quicksand. You feel like you're spinning out of control because you're without a secure axis. Be gentle with yourself, Tiff. God's got you, though it doesn't feel like it. He's pursuing you. He's got your back."

She turned to look at me with a questioning expression. "He does? I need you to keep telling me that. I don't know what to do about my kids. What do I tell them? How do I tell them? I know people who left the Church, but they're completely without faith and I don't want that. I want God in my life. But I don't have any idea what that looks like."

"I know it's so overwhelming and mysterious. I love that you want more of Jesus. He will keep leading you, Tiffanni. I promise. You'll walk into conversations with your kids in just the right time. You'll know when you need to know," I said.

"I believe that. This is so hard. On my mission, people would bring up the things I am learning about Joseph Smith as reasons that he isn't a true prophet of God. They brought up many issues with the historicity that I am learning about, but I was trained with ready defenses. I mindlessly defended Joseph and the Church with conviction. I never imagined I would be in this place."

"I get it, Tiffanni. I so get it. It is terrifying, but there is light at the end of this tunnel."

"There is? All I can see is the darkness. But you are giving me glimmers of light."

We had dodged the Florida mosquitos for an hour, and Tiffanni needed to put the kids to bed. With the comfort of an embrace, we returned to our homes.

Summer

As we entered into summer, Tiffanni shared with me that her husband was discontent with his job and had applied for a job back in Utah. My entire body felt the ache of that news. We were tasting the richness of sisterhood and a parallel journey in which so few people are able to share, because questioning Mormonism is such a unique experience. She had no desire to return to Utah. She was experiencing freedom in her search for answers because ward members weren't living all around her as they did in Utah, taking note of her every move. She was struggling with church attendance. When her family would decide to attend, she was met by some gracious members who didn't openly shame her for her unfaithful attendance. However, there were the faithful few who commented about her absence and couldn't hide their judgment.

After a four-week break from attending Young Women's on Wednesday nights with her teenage daughter, Tiffanni's daughter wanted to attend. When Tiffanni made her appearance, the Young Women's leader walked over to her and with a snide tone asked, "Where have you been? We've missed you. Are you going to be able to fulfill your calling to lead the Personal Progress night next Wednesday?"

This woman's whole being dripped with judgment. "I just want to go to a church where I can be completely anonymous!" Tiffanni told me. "I just want to show up and have no calling and nothing required of me for once in my life. No pressure. No guilt."

Because so much of her personal righteousness as a Mormon mom was attached to her faithful attendance to the various meetings and making sure her kids were at church on Sundays and during the week, she was failing miserably as a Mormon. Tiffanni had loved her life as a Mormon for many years. She had been a missionary, a gospel doctrine teacher, the Relief Society President (women's ministry), and had beautifully served in all her roles throughout her twenty-four years as a Mormon. However, as she was in this middle space of questioning, and feeling shame for doing so, there was enough distance for her to see and experience the costs of a performance-driven doctrine and how it trickles down into a community.

The more she thought about Jesus and His teachings, the more she gained an awareness of how Mormon doctrine was not aligned with the love, grace, and freedom His gospel brings. On the other hand, the more she researched the historicity of Mormonism, the more she was faced with realities about Mormonism that she couldn't reconcile. All of this worked together to make her question the standards of living that the Church required her to follow. For example, it lessened her conviction that it is holy and right to wear garments rather than pretty underwear—which would also allow her to put on a pair of short shorts occasionally.

A Trip to the Mall

Tiffanni and I were out one night when we decided to spontaneously stop by Ross Dress for Less at 10:00 p.m. As we were bantering about different pieces of clothing, she exclaimed, "Let's go pick out underwear for me!" Few people would feel the weight of her suggestion as strongly as I did. "Will you help me pick out pretty underwear?" Tiffanni asked.

"I would love to and I feel so honored to be with you on this premier shopping trip! I can't believe I get to do this with you. What a monumental event!" I exclaimed.

We rolled our carts to the back of the store and I gave her a tutorial on what makes an amazing pair of underwear amazing. As we sorted and shuffled through the racks, plentiful with options, we took turns spouting to each other about the rarity and gravity of this day. She was walking into the freedom that comes from the reality that God inhabits His followers and they are His temples. He isn't dependent upon the buildings that the Church calls temples to carry out special rituals and ordinances. Jesus had carried out all of the rituals necessary for eternal life. And so, that night at the town center, Tiffanni and I shared in the joy of outfitting her wardrobe with beautiful underwear, because she is His temple and is far more glorious than any building could be. This was one of those *stake-in-the-ground* events for Tiffanni, and I love that I got to be with her. On our ride back home that night, she mentioned, "I need to be careful that my kids don't see all of these yet, and I'm still not brave enough to wear short shorts in front of them." It is an interesting dynamic when religion creates an environment where so much emphasis is placed on these types of external dressings that a mom feels the need to hide underwear and shorts from her children in order to maintain equilibrium for them while she is in the eye of the storm. Yet, that is the extent to which a mom who is crazy over her kids will go in order to protect them from the storm that is turning her life upside down and inside out.

Still Unsettled

Tiffanni and I were at the gym one morning working out together when she shared, "I have a problem with the 'importance of the identity of God' idea you talked with me about in our first conversation—when I had that doubting look on my face."

"I could see that is a tough concept for you. Tell me your thoughts," I said.

"Mormons worship the Jesus of the Bible," she said. "They consider themselves Christians. They read about Jesus of Nazareth and believe that He is their Savior. They strive to live Christlike lives and follow the biblical Jesus. They just have all of the extra doctrines that cause them to have to strive for worthiness."

I listened carefully, then responded, "Here's the essence of the problem—Mormons do not believe in one God manifested in three persons, which is the biblical God. They believe Jesus was the offspring of Heavenly Father and Heavenly Mother in a preexisting world, and that He is our actual brother—and the brother of Satan. The biblical Jesus is begotten of the Father and is God. He wasn't created and He has always been God. He is not our actual brother, but can be our Lord and Savior. Even the Church website has an article clearly stating that the Church doesn't believe in the Christian view of God."[4]

"But they consider themselves Christians!" protested Tiffanni.

"I totally agree with you on that—they do consider themselves Christians," I said. "But these are not little doctrinal disagreements. These disagreements are about the identity of God Himself—and our identity, too. Back in the garden of Eden, God gave Adam and Eve one restriction—not to eat from the Tree of the Knowledge of Good and Evil. Do you remember what Adam and Eve wanted when they ate the fruit?" I asked.

Looking into Tiffanni's emotionally war-torn eyes, I waited for a response. She began to quote Scripture, which she knew well, working her mind through the passage in Genesis 2.

"They wanted to become like God, knowing good from evil," we said in tandem.

"They wanted to become like God. So they threw out living in the mysteries of His love and embraced a false vision of Him. They no longer saw God as He was, a faithful lover committed to their good. They replaced a correct view of Him with a skewed version of Him, that He is holding out on them and not committed to their good. This resulted in them choosing to take control of their destiny and become like God by eating from the Tree of the Knowledge of Good and Evil. Out of their skewed vision of His nature and identity, idolatry entered into this world. Now think about the end of goal of the Mormon plan of salvation. What is eternal life for a Mormon?"

"To become like God," Tiffanni replied in complete shock.

"Isn't it interesting that the entire goal of Mormonism is to exalt into godhood, which was the original sin?"

Tiffanni was completely shocked as she connected these dots. "I have never seen that before! How could I have never seen that and made the connection? This is crazy!"

"It is crazy, and Mormons, for some reason, cannot see it," I said.

"I just can't believe I never saw that!" Tiffanni again exclaimed.

Encompassed in Hope

Though Tiffanni would occasionally catch a ray of light in the dark tunnel she was navigating, she felt encompassed in darkness most of the time. A hopelessness rested on her as her curiosity gave way to disillusionment and an inability to envision the future. Her bed was a soft, comforting place to weather the especially dark days.

One week, after not touching base with Tiffanni for five days, I called her to see how she was doing. When she answered, she desperately began to share with me, "Lisa, I need you today. I've been in my house thinking I don't want to bother you, but I just need to go sit in a room with you where I can see you. I know you're writing your manuscript, but I don't even need to talk with you. I'll just sit in a corner and watch you type away on the computer. I just need to be in your calming presence!"

I exclaimed, "Tiffanni, you should have come over! And I wouldn't make you sit in a corner. I'd love for you to come be with me." Tiff couldn't wait to walk down to my home to unload the weight which had rested on her frightened shoulders and heart all morning. Instead of taking the time to do that, we continued our conversation on the phone.

"Lisa, my husband was offered the job in Utah. I don't want to move back there. What am I doing going back to Utah? What am I going to do when none of my friends want to be my friend anymore?" Tiffanni asked with incredible angst.

We sat in silence for a bit. There aren't any pat answers to those stirrings of her heart. I then I offered with deep conviction, "Jesus will be with you, my friend."

Desperately she said, "He'll be with me, right? And He's enough. If He's the only friend I have, He's enough. Right?"

"Yes, He is enough." I assured her from personal experience. Then I added, "You will be supported, Tiff. I will hook you up with some good people who understand what you are going through and will walk alongside you."

"I don't want to move all of our stuff all the way across the country again. We just did that seven months ago, and the sound of it makes me anxious. I don't know how this is all going to work out. I don't know when to put our house on the market," she said.

"You can put your house on the market now or you can put it on the market in January. You can rest in the reality that God is in control if you allow Him to be, and He is good and kind. Your house will sell in His timing."

"I know that's true," said Tiffanni as her voice welled up with emotion, "but I'm struggling so much believing that He's near. I just hear I'm unworthy and not worthy of His love or presence or help."

"Tiffanni, let me share a verse from the Bible that I read this morning to remind you of who the biblical God is.

"'Listen to me, family of Jacob [I inserted Tiff's name], everyone that's left of the family of Israel. I've been carrying you on my back from the day you were born, and I'll keep on carrying you when you're old. I'll be there, bearing you when you're old and gray. I've done it and will keep on doing it, carrying you on my back, saving you' (Isaiah 46:3-4 MSG)."

> It is a treacherous journey walking out of the Temple into the shadows.

I choked my way through the verse. The reality of the tender faithfulness of the biblical God broke through the stress, the fatigue, and the fear in Tiffanni's soul and tears poured forth, soothing her fearful heart.

"That's who He is. That Scripture grounds me right now like none other," she said.

"Yes, that is who He is. He's been carrying you on His back since the day you were born and will keep doing so until you're old and gray. He's never left you and won't forsake you."

The dam broke in Tiffanni's soul. Soft tears traveled through the phone line—tears of relief that God was with her. She tasted God's huge heart for her and believed His unconditional love and faithfulness to be true for the first time. As I sat on the other end of the line, tears rolled down my face that my treasured friend was tasting and seeing the deep love of the biblical God.

It is a treacherous journey walking out of the Temple into the shadows. It is a complete reorientation in the midst of the thickest possible fog of disillusionment. There is no more certainty of what is real. Certainty is replaced with a skepticism that another God could be that good, that faithful, and that loving as to never leave you. Some post-Mormons end up believing that a God like this exists, but it seems, for more apostates than not, it is too far of a stretch to believe.

Lipstick Says It All

The following day, Tiffanni called me mid-morning and said she was coming over to talk. I love a friend who feels the freedom to do that. When I opened the door a few minutes later, she was standing there in her forest green shirt and jeans, with her long, flowy hair, looking completely energized. I couldn't wait to hear what had happened inside of her to move her from the utter despair I had witnessed the day before to this space of freedom.

"I just got off the phone with David, the man who was like a father to me when I was in my twenties."

"Oh good, I'm so glad you connected with him. What happened on your call?"

"He's a very influential psychiatrist globally and has posted regularly on Facebook for years. Four years ago, I noticed that his spiritual quotes weren't using Mormon jargon anymore and were simpler. It was an obvious shift, which I haven't talked with him about because we haven't been in touch with each other."

"I can't wait to hear! Tell me what you discovered," I said.

"I shared with him about my crisis of faith that began a year ago, what I've been discovering about the Church and its history, and how I'm in turmoil over it. I told him all about you and how you're pointing me to the biblical Jesus. I talked to him about my family and my kids and how I don't have any idea how to navigate this path."

"How did he respond to you?" I asked. She looked as if a thousand-pound weight had been lifted from her shoulders.

"David said that his faith crisis happened four years ago. I knew something had happened in him! He said that he read about the Book of Abraham and learned that Joseph had claimed the Egyptian hieroglyphs told the story of that book. But when experts determined that the hieroglyphs were actually telling the story of an Egyptian burial ceremony, his faith in Mormonism was shot. He said that his wife experienced her faith crisis alongside him and together they, along with all of their children, have left Mormonism."

David compassionately shared his story with Tiffanni and was the encourager she needed at this point in her journey. She needed to see from a recently departed post-Mormon whom she respects and adores that living a life of faith in Jesus Christ is possible outside of Mormonism. After hearing for over twenty years that "the Church is true" and has the fullness of the gospel, whereas every other religion or church only possesses partial truth, it is like climbing Mount Everest to entertain the thought of attending another church or participating in another faith community.

As we sat at my kitchen table with the sun beaming in the windows behind Tiff, I delighted in God's pursuit of my friend. He was so kind and attentive to her in her darkness and desolation. I was privileged to watch hope be birthed in her soul and it was springing to life before my eyes. I had known Tiffanni for six short months, and this was the first day since I had met her where hope seemed to pour forth from inside of her.

As Tiffanni came to the end of her story with David that morning, she exclaimed, "Lisa, when you read that verse from Isaiah to me yesterday—that was the moment of my reconversion to Jesus! Heavenly Father restored my faith! You are a missionary and I want to be a missionary like you!"

I couldn't contain my joy over the transformation that was occurring in my friend's entire being. Tiff embodied faith rooted and grounded in the love of the biblical God, and her joy spilled forth.

"I love how God is relentlessly pursuing you! You are a different person today than the woman I've journeyed alongside the past six months," I shared.

"I am. I know I am loved and enough because Jesus is in me. I even wrote that on my vanity mirror in lipstick. 'I am enough.' Jesus made me worthy and I am free. I wonder if Heavenly Father is taking us back to Utah so that I can lead Mormons and post-Mormons to the biblical Jesus. I want them to experience this freedom."

I walked Tiffanni down the street, a bit more hope filling her than when she had arrived. One of the sweetest gifts of journeying with her has been continually pouring the mercy and grace of the biblical God over her. I watch His love transform her heart in front of my eyes each time we are together.

Tiffanni's story continues to unfold with twists and turns. Our time together was short, but the connection and sisterhood we enjoy is rare and priceless. She has a long road ahead of her filled with mystery, but she is clinging to the hand of Jesus with the confidence of His unwavering presence.

My relationship with Tiffanni is a rare one. I have journeyed with my family and other Mormons for twenty-seven years and enjoyed very few doctrinal conversations with them. There is no formula for journeying with people. It is always a gift to love and be loved, whatever the landscape. However, journeying with Tiffanni has been sheer joy because of her courage, vulnerability, and honesty. Her family has just moved back to Utah, which tears at our hearts. It has been a surreal gift from God for us both to have each other to journey with this year. God is without question the kindest and most intentional pursuer I have ever known.

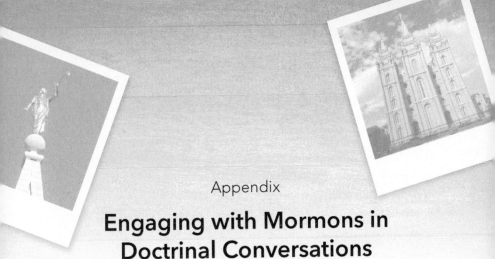

Engaging with Mormons in Doctrinal Conversations

Jesus on the cross didn't try to talk the two thieves into anything—it was one of them who turned to him![1]

DIETRICH BONHOEFFER

Early in our friendship, Tiffanni shared with me a story about an encounter she had with a neighbor in Utah who was a Christian. One day, Tiffanni offered to make their family dinner. She rang the doorbell with hands full of food, and her neighbor greeted her with one hand behind her back. When she turned around to lead Tiffanni into the house, Tiff saw that it was a book about how to share Christ with Mormons. It is safe to say she was not feeling the love of her Christian neighbor at that moment. I think it is wonderful that her neighbor desired to be more effective in communicating the biblical gospel to her Mormon neighbors. However, greeting them with the resource in hand is not the most loving way to go about it. Jesus said that people will know His followers by their love. I believe and have experienced this to be a reality.

Everyone is on a spiritual journey of some kind, even if they don't believe in God. Being invited into a person's journey is one of the greatest gifts I know. Several years ago, Dennis and I sat across from my little brother and his wife and asked them if they would share their journey with Mormonism, and their struggle with their beliefs with us. They were in the middle of a faith crisis, and we wanted to journey with them in any way possible. Matt and his wife, Megan, shared their journeys with authenticity and vulnerability. We were curious about the impact their faith crisis was having on their relationships with God and others.

As Matt came to the close of his story, he said, "I don't know where I will land in the end. I don't know what I will believe or if I will be in a church or not. But what I do know is that wherever I land and whatever I believe, you will always love me." Matt could not have offered us a higher compliment. I had not had one doctrinal conversation with Matt since I had left Mormonism decades earlier, but I had embodied the mercy and grace and unconditional love and acceptance that the biblical God has poured into me, which I delighted in pouring into them. I sought to embody the gospel and my brother felt embraced.

When seeking to share the biblical Jesus with Mormons, may love be the undercurrent upon which all of your words flow. Love is patient and kind and bold and gentle and honest. It does not force itself on others. I have not had doctrinal conversations with the majority of my family members since I began following the biblical Jesus. The invitation has rarely presented itself. However, I have been blessed to live a life of love with them, as well as to receive their love. But, when there have been openings and invitations, I seek to engage those with grace and truth, speaking in their native language. Sometimes this is challenging, but it is my intention.

Speaking Their Dialect

Nelson Mandela said, "If you talk to a man in a language he understands, that goes to his head. If you talk to him in his language, that goes to his heart." The essence of this quote is my motivation for writing *Out of Zion*. I long for people to enter into the soul freedom that Jesus Christ is continually offering us. I especially long for Mormons to taste this freedom. Because Mormonism is not merely a religion, but a culture, you will not enjoy much success in doctrinal conversations with Mormons if you don't speak their native language. I hope reading *Out of Zion* has increased your understanding of Mormon culture and language so that you might enjoy doctrinal conversations with them. The reason I place so much emphasis on the plan of salvation is because this is the essence of the journey for people who believe in God. There are so many doctrinal differences between Mormonism and historical biblical Christianity that it can be difficult to know where to "land the plane" in conversation. There are significant issues with Mormonism's historicity and the authenticity of Joseph Smith as a true prophet of God. There are excellent resources available on these topics, and it is good to understand them.[2] But, for an active Mormon who is not open to exploration, those topics are not their native tongue, and they will erect a wall at the mere mention of them. As a result, my approach to conversing with Mormons is centered around the biblical and Mormon plans of salvation. These other topics are important to address at some point, but learning about them does not bring a Mormon hope. I believe that Jesus is the hope of the world and so I keep bringing the conversation back to Him.

One characteristic that was true of me as a Mormon, and is true of every Mormon I know, is that they are adamant that they are Christians. What I also know from experience is that I did not know that the biblical plan of salvation was any different from the Mormon plan of salvation. I was young and sheltered and had not been educated about this. Many you encounter will not have a clear understanding of the biblical plan of salvation or the biblical God, concepts that are critical to defining a Christian. They believe they have clear vision of these things and will take great offense if you tell them otherwise. There is a one-up posturing that comes from believing that only they have the *fullness of the gospel*. Other Christians are living on partial revelation in their minds. My goal when talking with Mormon missionaries is to help them see what the biblical plan of salvation is, and to point out that it is a very different plan, with a very different purpose for people than the Mormon plan. In addition, it is the biblical plan of salvation and belief in the biblical God (one God manifested in three persons) that makes one a Christian.

It is critical to speak to Mormons in their language and know how they define key terms, like salvation and eternal life, and how those definitions differ from biblical definitions. So, let's dive into my charts on pages 194 and 195 that parallel the Mormon and biblical plans of salvation.

When the doorbell rings and you open it up to two young men in suits and ties or women in skirts and blouses (or dress pants—which is finally allowed), with name badges beginning with *Elder* or *Sister*, you know you are in the presence of Mormon missionaries. That knock on the door may cause an array of emotions. There have been times when the missionaries were at my door and I ducked down out of sight in my bathrobe. There have been other times when I am glad to invite them into our home and invite them to stay for dinner. All that I offer is a short one-minute overview of my story from Mormon girl to Christ-following woman. There have also been times when we engage in long doctrinal conversations. The one thing that is true of every encounter with a Mormon missionary is they are extending an invitation to join them in a conversation.

Where to Begin

Because personal testimony is the Mormon's plumb line for knowing that their Church is true, I begin by asking them if they would be willing to share their testimony with me. I want to hear about their encounter with a burning in the bosom, which moved them into a place of knowing. Missionaries are glad to share their testimonies, and it is a place for you to enter into their story with curiosity. Get to know them and how they ended up at your front door. Discover what their testimonies mean to them.

After they finish sharing their testimonies, offer to share your testimony with them. After you share yours, you will be at a place in the conversation where you all have expressed that you have encountered God in some way. This encounter brought about a conviction that what you believe is true. But Mormonism and biblical Christianity are two very different belief systems that make it unrealistic for them both to be true. I have said to missionaries, "There must be another way of determining truth than personal testimony, since we both are confident about the truthfulness of our beliefs, but they're not the same. Let's explore the biblical plan of salvation and the Mormon plan of salvation."

Plans of Salvation

I would ask the missionaries to share with you the main details of the Mormon plan of salvation. You might draw a line graph as they share. They likely will avoid sharing details that don't sound like mainstream Christianity. One of these would be that they believe we were all offspring of Heavenly Father and Heavenly Mother, birthed in a preexisting world. Their purpose for coming to this earth is to gain a mortal body under the banner of free agency. Here they have the opportunity to exalt into godhood, like Heavenly Father did, if they've been faithful to keep the laws and ordinances of the Mormon gospel. The essentials elements to cover are:

1. Who is God? What is His nature?

2. Who are we? What is our nature?

3. Why are we here? For what are we designed?

4. Where are we going?

5. How do we get there?

Give the missionaries the floor. Listen and repeat back to them what you are hearing to make sure you understand their language and definition of terms. I think it is most helpful to draw this out in a time line, as in the charts on pages 194 and 195. This is not a time to debate, but rather, to seek understanding and not get bogged down in any one area. If they are not sharing that their purpose here is to make themselves worthy for eternal life through their Temple marriage and exaltation into godhood in the Celestial Kingdom, then ask them about it. That is their end goal and purpose. The key elements of the Mormon plan of salvation are:

1. *Our beginning*: People came from a preexisting world where Heavenly Father and Heavenly Mother begot us as spirit intelligences. Jesus was the firstborn of us all and our brother—not God. Lucifer (Satan) was also our brother.

2. *Our nature*: We came to this earth with a divine nature, rather than a sinful nature. Jesus's death washes away Adam's sin from everyone, whether they receive Him or not.

3. *Baptism*: This washes away any sins we have committed while on the earth previous to the baptism, and is the first ordinance required in eternal progression into godhood.

4. *Making ourselves worthy for eternal life*: We are to obey the laws and ordinances of the gospel (i.e., baptism, regular church attendance and activity, obeying the Word of Wisdom, paying a full tithe, a Temple marriage, Temple work—faithfully doing all of these things throughout their lives) with the hope that we will make ourselves worthy for eternal life, which is exaltation into godhood in the Celestial Kingdom.

5. *Eternity*: If we have made ourselves worthy for a Temple marriage and have remained faithful to the laws and ordinances of the Mormon gospel, we will likely make it into the Celestial Kingdom, where we would be in the presence of Heavenly Father and Jesus Christ and the Holy Ghost. There we would remain married to our earthly spouse throughout eternity and would exalt into gods and goddesses/queens/high priestesses and rule our own kingdoms. The women will birth spirit children throughout eternity and often reside in polygamous marriages.

Share the Biblical Plan of Salvation

Now it is your turn to draw the biblical plan of salvation. The key elements of the biblical plan are:

1. *Our beginning*: The biblical God consists of three persons—Father, Son, and Spirit— who have existed in a perfect community of love at the center of the universe from eternity to eternity. Because of Their self-giving nature, They desired to draw others into Their community. They created us to live in Their community of love (the kingdom of God), in which They desire to fill us with Their love to overflowing, so that we may pour it back into Them and others. We were created to image God, reflecting the love, grace, and stewardship of God in this world. Being made in the image of God means that we are relational beings who are designed with a call and capacity to rule and govern the earth in a way that reflects His love, power, goodness, and grace. We didn't come from a preexisting world and were not begotten of God and a Heavenly Mother. (The Mormon narrative is that there is not any mention of her because Heavenly Father does not want her name taken in vain.)

2. *Our nature*: We are born with a sinful nature, not a divine nature. We are participants in the sin of Adam and Eve, thus we are born spiritually dead, and not in relationship with God. We look to created things to be our axis around which we spin, looking for love, life, and significance in these rather than in God (idolatry). Because of sin, our image-bearing vocation fractures. Sin, meaning "missing the mark," is missing the mark of true humanness. When we worship idols (anything other than the God of the universe), we give a part of our power and glory to the idol and diminish our humanness.

We were created to image God in this world (not literally as flesh and bones as the Mormons interpret that verse). We were created with the glorious task of reflecting God's power and love into this world. We were meant to be agents of God's new creation, to model and display it in the arts and in family life, in restorative justice and in creativity, in service to the poor and in politics. We were designed as agents and stewards of God's great universe. We were created to be people of beauty through whom fresh beauty comes into this world.

3. *Salvation/eternal life begins*: At our point of conversion, we accept that we have a sinful nature and are unable to save ourselves. We place our trust in Christ's sacrifice for our sins because we know we are in need of redemption and cannot provide the perfect sacrifice for ourselves. We trust in His righteousness. At this point, we walk into the kingdom of God. Eternal life has begun. He promises He will never leave us or forsake us. He seals us with His Holy Spirit—pours His Spirit into us and the Spirit never leaves us. We are His children and have begun living eternal life (life with God in His kingdom with the capacity to transform into the glorious likeness of Jesus Christ) at this point. We are part of the bride of Christ, which consists of all Christ-followers. This is what Ephesians 2:8-9 means, "For by grace you have been saved through faith. And this is not your own doing; it is the gift of God, not a result of works, so that no one may boast." *It is important to note that biblically, saved/salvation=eternal life.* Mormons always say, "We believe that it is by grace we are saved," because they have redefined salvation as overcoming death and resurrecting to one of the three Heavens of Mormon doctrine: Celestial, Telestial, and Terrestrial Kingdoms or Outer Darkness. According to Mormon doctrine,

salvation is not eternal life—in the presence of the Father, Son, and Spirit throughout eternity. Exaltation to godhood in a marriage to one's earthly spouse in the Celestial Kingdom is eternal life according to Mormon doctrine. *This is a significant and critical distinction between Christianity and Mormonism.*

4. *Baptism*: This is an outward expression of an inward reality. We have allowed God to put to death our sinful nature and are now alive to God because we trust in Jesus's sacrifice for us.

5. *Life in God's kingdom*: Once we walk into God's kingdom, we are invited to begin living a with-God life (eternal life). God made us worthy through Jesus and that is unchanging. He empowers us to grow through His Spirit, who takes up permanent residence within us. Because He lives in us, the divine life of Christ is alive and active in our souls. He desires intimacy with us and wants to transform us into the image-bearers that He designed us to be, as well as to bring us to rest in His care and provision for us. God invites us into a life of transformation for our good and His glory, not to make us worthy of His love, acceptance, presence, and exaltation. He doesn't force Himself on us because love doesn't force itself on another. But He is always there awaiting our invitation to deeper intimacy, and transforming us into the others-centered lovers He designed us to be. This transformation enables us to reflect His image more vividly and accurately on the earth, which was His original design. As we grow into the image-bearers He created us to be, we become more fully the humans He designed us to be.

6. *Eternity*: At our physical death, we have the gift of assurance that we will be in the presence of the Trinity throughout

eternity for we have been living in His kingdom since placing our trust in Christ. The difference is that we will be made perfect, and there will be nothing separating us from God's presence. We will be the bride of Christ throughout eternity, not married to our earthly spouses.

After articulating the biblical plan of salvation, I say to the missionaries, "I have eternal life and it began the day I walked into God's kingdom by placing my trust in Christ for eternal life. I am a member of Christ's Church universal, which is the bride of Christ, the God of the universe. I will reign with Him throughout eternity (2 Timothy 2:11-13). What do you have to offer me that I don't already enjoy?"

Usually, the missionaries are speechless because they do not have anything to offer me that I do not enjoy as a Christian. One time when I was going through the plans of salvation with two kind sister missionaries, I posed this question at the end of our time and they were without words. After a minute, one of them responded in a questioning tone, "A Temple marriage?" Compassion filled my heart for them as they dug deep for some answer that would validate their beliefs.

I responded, "Jesus Christ, who is the God of the universe, is the husband of His Church universal, to which I belong. Why would I want or need an earthly husband eternally when I am part of the bride of Christ, the God of the universe?"

Again, they were speechless. I gently asked them, "What happens if you don't get a Temple marriage? Have you considered what that would mean for you?"

They had not considered it. I invited them to wrestle with the reality that if they are one of the unfortunate Mormon women who do not marry in the Temple, their ability to exalt to their highest degree of glory is compromised. My heart ached for them as I walked them to the door, hoping that they had caught a vision of the biblical God and the beliefs that make a Christian a Christian.

After we have established that Mormonism is not Christianity, we can delve deeper into each part of the plan of salvation in future meetings, if there happen to be any. I have found that the missionaries do not return for a second visit after we have worked through the plans of salvation. My hope is that I pricked something in their hearts that will keep coming back to them, so that if they come to a place in their lives when they hunger for a freedom that Mormonism cannot offer them, they will remember in whom they can find that freedom.

When you are in long-term relationship with Mormons, it is less likely that you will have the opportunity to sit down with them upon first meeting or for some time after and do this exercise with the plans of salvation. Your journey will be more organic as you wait for an invitation while building a friendship. However, if you have this grid in your mind, then when doors open for doctrinal conversation, you have the tools in your toolbox to speak to the person or persons in their native tongue.

Avoiding Pitfalls

Faith without works is dead: One of the Bible verses that Mormons like to use to present their case for a works-based eternal life is from James 2:26 (KJV), "For as the body without the spirit is dead, so faith without works is dead also." I like to respond by saying, "I absolutely agree with that. The difference between our beliefs is that faith will manifest in good works—they naturally flow out of a love relationship with God. However, good works will not produce faith. Faith must be the origin out of which our works flow. Otherwise, our good works are to gain something rather than an outflow of grace.

We believe that we're saved by grace: Make clear that salvation and eternal life are one and the same, biblically speaking. Salvation is not merely resurrecting from the grave, as Mormon doctrine claims, but is eternal life in the presence of the Father, Son, and Holy Spirit. Ask what they must do in order to receive eternal life. If they're being honest, they must admit they need a Temple marriage. Then I would ask them what they must do to be worthy of a Temple marriage.

✝ Biblical Plan of Salvation

God has existed in a perfect community of love as Father, Son, and Holy Spirit from eternity to eternity. He created us to share in His love and to be God-imagers—reflecting His love, stewardship, and grace in the world.

"In the beginning was the Word, and the Word was with God, and the Word was God" (John 1:1 NIV).

Birth
We are created in the image of God and beloved by Him. Our nature is sinful and we are spiritually dead (Psalm 139:13; Romans 6:23).

Trust Christ
Spiritual birth/new nature given; God pours His Spirit into believers, sealing them to Him. Eternal life with God begins and continues throughout eternity. God's grace through Christ provides us assurance of our eternal destiny with the Father, Son, and Holy Spirit (Ephesians 2:8-9; 1 John 5:11-13).

Reject Christ

Growing in Christlikeness
Spiritual transformation/good works flow out of God's love for us and are an invitation to partner with Him in what He is doing in the world (2 Corinthians 5:17, Colossians 3:1-17).

Death

Death

A New Heaven and a New Earth
In the new heaven and new earth, we live in the perfection of God's kingdom—in the circle of love of the Father, Son, and Holy Spirit. We are the bride of Christ and will reign with Him throughout eternity (John 17:24; Revelation 21).

Hell
The state for those who did not desire or accept God's invitation to live with Him eternally during their earthly life will be granted their desire to spend eternity outside of His kingdom (Matthew 8:12; 2 Thessalonians 1:9).

Mormon Plan of Salvation

> "We remember the numerous scriptures which, concentrated in a single line, were said by a former prophet, Lorenzo Snow. 'As man is, God once was; and as God is, man may become.' This is a power available to us as we reach perfection and receive the experience and power to create, to organize, to control native elements. How limited we are now! We have no power to force the grass to grow, the plants to emerge, the seeds to develop."–Spencer W. Kimball, General Conference, April 1977
>
> *"We know that it is by grace we are saved, after all we can do"* (2 Nephi 25:23).

Preexistence
All people were birthed as spirit children in a preexisting world as offspring of Heavenly Father and Heavenly Mother, giving people a divine nature (Moses 3:5).

Veil of Forgetfulness

Birth
We are born with a divine nature and come to earth to gain a physical body with free agency to choose between good and evil. Jesus gives everyone salvation from birth—the ability to resurrect from the grave.

Baptism/Holy Ghost
The Holy Ghost does not indwell Mormons but visits according to one's worthiness. Baptism is necessary to enter the Mormon Temple and gain eternal life (2 Nephi 31:17-18).

Life Outside the Mormon Church

Death

Working Out Salvation
"It is by grace that we are saved, after all we can do" (2 Nephi 25:23).

Apostasy

Spirit World
Prison (hell) for the unrighteous, who are being proselytized to accept the Mormon gospel.

Death

Death

Spirit World
A paradise of happiness, rest, and peace for the righteous.

Accept Mormonism

Reject Mormonism

Resurrection and Last Judgment

Resurrection and Last Judgment

Resurrection and Last Judgment

Celestial Kingdom
There are three levels and only Temple-married Mormons receive the highest degree of glory and exalt into angels or gods. This is the place of eternal life with Heavenly Father and Jesus Christ, who reside here.

Outer Darkness
Apostates and murderers will suffer the wrath of God with the devil and his angels forever.

Terrestrial Kingdom
The good and honorable but blinded by the craftiness of men; accepted Mormonism in the post-mortal spirit world. Jesus visits this level of heaven.

Telestial Kingdom
The dishonest, liars, sorcerers, adulterers, and whoremongers; rejected Mormonism on earth and in the spirit prison; toured hell but have been redeemed to the lowest heaven. Christ doesn't visit this level of heaven.

1st Level
Baptism

2nd Level
Endowments

3rd Level
Temple Marriage

Notes

A Note on Names

1. Scott Taylor, "Name of the Church 'Not Negotiable,' President Nelson Says" *Church News and Events*, October 7, 2018, www.lds.org/church/news/name-of-the-church-not-negotiable-president-nelson-says.

Chapter 1—When One Question Shakes the Whole Foundation

1. Barbara Brown Taylor, *Learning to Walk in the Dark* (New York: HarperCollins, 2014), 67.
2. *Doctrine and Covenants* 9:8-9.
3. LDS Article of Faith 1:8.

Chapter 2—The Great Plan of Happiness

1. Dan Allender, *To Be Told* (Colorado Springs: Waterbrook Press, 2005), 64.
2. See Mosiah 18:8–10; *Doctrine and Covenants* 20:37.
3. The language used was that we could become gods. I translated this to goddess because I was a girl. Mormon language also refers to women exalting into queens and high priestesses to their husbands who are their gods. Whatever the term, we would exalt into deity.
4. "Sacrament," accessed April 30, 2019, https://www.lds.org/topics/sacrament.
5. Handbook 2.2, *Administering the Church*, "Music in the Ward" (section 14.4) and "Sacrament Meetings" (section 14.4.4), March 2019, www.lds.org/study/manual/handbook-2-administering-the-church/music/music.
6. Grant Von Harrison, *Understanding Your Divine Nature* (Woods Cross, UT: Publishers Book Sales, 1985), 111–12.
7. Von Harrison, *Understanding Your Divine Nature*, 105.
8. Brigham Young, *Discourses of Brigham Young* (Salt Lake City, UT: Deseret Book Co., 1941), 88.

Chapter 3—Worthy

1. Jean Vanier, *Seeing Beyond Depression* (Mahwah, NJ: Paulist Press, 2001), 29.
2. Dieter Uchtdorf, "The Power of a Personal Testimony," *The Church of Jesus Christ of Latter-day Saints*, October 2006, https://www.lds.org/general-conference/2006/10/the-power-of-a-personal-testimony.

3. *Doctrine and Covenants* 88:118.

4. Brigham Young, "A Discourse by President Brigham Young, Delivered in the Tabernacle, Great Salt Lake City, June 13th, 1852," *Journal of Discourses* 1 (90), http://jod.mrm.org/1/88.

5. Heber J. Grant, Conference Report, Oct. 1929, pages 4-5, quoted in Dallin H. Oaks, "Tithing," www.lds.org/general-conference/1994/04/tithing.

6. Spencer W. Kimball, "President Kimball Speaks Out on Tithing," *The Church of Jesus Christ of Latter-day Saints,* April 1981, www.lds.org/new-era/1981/04/president-kimball-speaks-out-on-tithing.

7. Shanna Butler, "What Happened to Christ's Church?" *Liahona,* www.lds.org/liahona/2005/02/what-happened-to-christs-church.

8. David A. Bednar, "The Powers of Heaven." *The Church of Jesus Christ of Latter-day Saints,* www.lds.org/general-conference/2012/04/the-powers-of-heaven?lang=eng.

9. *Pearl of Great Price,* Moses 7:22.

10. Bruce R. McConkie, "All Are Alike unto God." *BYU Speeches,* August 18, 1978, speeches.byu.edu/talks/bruce-r-mcconkie_alike-unto-god-2/.

11. *Doctrine and Covenants* 1:14–16.

12. "A Mormon Bishop Talks About Interviewing Youth," *Mormon Hub,* December 21, 2017, mormonhub.com/blog/community-contribution/momon-bishop-talks-interviewing-youth/.

Chapter 4– From Pebbles to Boulders

1. Tim Keller, "The Grace of the Law," *Redeemer Report,* January 2009, www.redeemer.com/redeemer-report/article/the_grace_of_the_law.

2. *Doctrine and Covenants* 115:5.

3. Alma 39:5.

4. Von Harrison, *Understanding Your Divine Nature,* 91.

5. Spencer W. Kimball, "The Importance of Celestial Marriage," *Ensign,* www.lds.org/ensign/1979/10/the-importance-of-celestial-marriage.

6. *Doctrine and Covenants* 89.

Chapter 5– Breaking Free from Shame's Straitjacket

1. Eugene Peterson, *Leap Over a Wall: Earthy Spirituality for Everyday Christians* (New York: Harper Collins, 1997), 99–100.

2. "Mormonism Says God Impregnated Mary by Sex," *BeliefMap,* accessed January 30, 2019, https://beliefmap.org/mormonism/mormonism-teaches-god-and-mary-sexually-produced-jesus.

3. See *Doctrine and Covenants* 132. According to Peggy Fletcher Stack, "Polygamy is still enshrined in LDS scripture. In his quasi-official 1966 book Mormon Doctrine, which remains in print, the late LDS Apostle Bruce R. McConkie wrote that 'the holy practice will commence again after the Second Coming and the ushering in of the millennium.' And by policy, men can be 'sealed' for eternity in LDS Temple rites to more than one wife, though women are permitted only a single sealing. Three of the church's current apostles, for example, were widowed and remarried. Each will have two wives in the eternities." See "Modern-Day Mormons Disavow Polygamy," *Salt Lake Tribune,* April 20, 2008, http://archive.sltrib.com/article.php?id=8989865&itype=NGPSID.

4. "Virtue," *The Church of Jesus Christ of Latter-day Saints,* accessed January 30, 2019, www.lds.org/young-women/personal-progress/virtue.

Chapter 6– Exploring the Web

1. Margaret Atwood, *Alias Grace* (London: Bloomsbury Publishing, 1996), 298.

2. *Doctrine and Covenants* 130:22.

3. Lorenzo Snow, *Teachings of the Presidents of the Church: Lorenzo Snow* (Salt Lake City, UT: The Church of Jesus Christ of Latter-day Saints, 2012), from Chapter 5, "The Grand Destiny of the Faithful."

4. I was taught in church that we would become gods in the Celestial Kingdom. I translated this to goddess in my case because I was a girl. The language the church uses in one of their ceremonies is queen and high priestess to my husband, who would be a god. One way or the other, I would exalt into deity.

5. All quotations in this paragraph are taken from *Doctrine and Covenants* 76:73–106.

6. In *Dialogue: A Journal of Mormon Thought*, LDS professor Dee Green wrote, "The first myth we need to eliminate is that Book of Mormon archaeology exists" (1969, pages 74-78).

7. Sean McDowell, "What Is the Most Recent Manuscript Count for the New Testament?" May 23, 2018, www.seanmcdowell.org/blog/what-is-the-most-recent-manuscript-count-for -the-new-testament.

8. This topic is discussed extensively in the CES letter, a document containing Jeremy Runnells'(a Mormon at the time) questions to the Church Education System as he confronted many historical issues with the Mormon Church.

9. Jeremy Runnells, *CES Letter CES Letter: My Search for Answers to My Mormon Doubts* (April 2013, updated October 2017), https://cesletter.org/CES-Letter.pdf., 52-56.

10. Ibid.

11. This is the classic "Liar, Lunatic, or Lord" argument first put forth by John Duncan and popularized by C. S. Lewis.

Chapter 7– A Portal into Another Reality

1. Iain Matthew, *The Impact of God: Soundings from St. John of the Cross* (London: Hodder & Stoughton, 1995), 146.

2. I later discovered that this phrase comes from Revelation 4.

Chapter 9– Stunning Surrender

1. Anne Lamott, *Traveling Mercies: Some Thoughts on Faith* (New York: Anchor Books, 1999), 143.

Chapter 10– Tumultuous Waters

1. Dan Allender, *To Be Told* (Colorado Springs: Waterbrook Press, 2005), 17.

2. Joseph Smith's first vision in which he claims to have encountered God the Father and His Son, Jesus Christ, is what inspired Joseph to establish the Church of Jesus Christ of Latter-day Saints.

3. "The Testimony of the Prophet Joseph Smith." *Ensign*, www.lds.org/topics/joseph-smith/ testimony.

Chapter 11– To Have and to Hold

1. Richard Rohr, *What the Mystics Know* (New York: The Crossroad Publishing Company, 2015), 104.

Chapter 12– Journeying with Tiffanni

1. Larry Crabb, *Shattered Dreams* (Colorado Springs: WaterBrook Press, 2001), 63.

2. Mayberry is a fictitious North Carolina town which was the setting for *The Andy Griffith Show* in the 1960's. It represents going back in time fifty years when society was slower, simpler, and less progressive.

3. Every church member is called to fill a position—or calling—in the church each year, and there isn't much freedom to decline without shame.

4. Peterson, Daniel C., and Stephen D. Ricks. *Comparing LDS Beliefs with First-Century Christianity*, www.lds.org/study/ensign/1988/03/comparing-lds-beliefs-with-first-century-christianity.

Appendix

1. Dietrich Bonhoeffer, *Letters and Papers from Prison* (New York: Simon and Schuster, 1997), 261.

2. As a starting place, I recommend looking at Jeremy Runnells' *CES Letter: My Search for Answers to My Mormon Doubts* (April 2013, updated October 2017), https://cesletter.org/CES-Letter.pdf.

Lisa Brockman is married to Dennis and is a mother of five passionate kids. She is a twenty-seven-year missionary with Cru, a spiritual director, and has graduated from Renovaré Institute for Christian Spiritual Formation. She was raised in a devout Mormon family in Salt Lake City, Utah and adores them. She attended East High, the film site of *High School Musical*—a small claim to fame. She feels spoiled to have lived in Florida the past twenty-six years. Lisa loves journeying with people through their spiritual highs, lows, and wanderings, and is passionate about people encountering the biblical God, who promises a love and freedom that has revolutionized her life. She loves to create tantalizing culinary creations for her family and friends, where they spend endless hours at the table sharing life and stories. The beach is her oasis.

While attending the University of Utah, she began dating Gary, a baseball player who called himself a Christian. This relationship catapulted her into a search she had never envisioned for her life. In her determination to prove the truth of Mormonism, she was introduced to the love and grace of the biblical God, who radically changed the trajectory of her life.

To learn more about Harvest House books and
to read sample chapters, visit our website:

www.harvesthousepublishers.com

HARVEST HOUSE PUBLISHERS
EUGENE, OREGON